Sometimes I Wake Up GRUMPY...

and Sometimes I Let Him Sleep

Other books by Karen Scalf Linamen

Protecting Your Child through Prayer

Welcome to the Funny Farm: The All-True Misadventures of a Woman on the Edge

Harried with Children

Just Hand Over the Chocolate and No One Will Get Hurt

Pillow Talk

I'm Not Suffering from Insanity . . . I'm Enjoying Every Minute of It!

Sometimes I Wake Up GRUMPY ...

and Sometimes I Let Him Sleep

KAREN SCALF LINAMEN

Revell
Grand Rapids, Michigan

© 2001 by Karen Scalf Linamen

Published by Fleming H. Revell
a division of Baker Publishing Group
P.O. Box 6287, Grand Rapids, MI 49516-6287

Sixth printing, February 2005

Printed in the United States of America

Library of Congress Cataloging-in-Publication Data
Linamen, Karen Scalf, 1960–
    Sometimes I wake up grumpy—and sometimes I let him sleep / Karen Scalf Linamen.
        p.   cm.
    ISBN 0-8007-5745-9 (pbk.)
    1. Man-woman relationships. 2. Women—Psychology. 3. Women—Conduct of life. 4. Family. I. Title.
HQ801.L472 2001
306.7—dc21   00-066504

Scripture is from the King James Version of the Bible.

Some material in chapter 9 is taken from the September/October 1997 issue of *Today's Christian Woman.*

For my daughters, Kaitlyn and Kacie, who have yet to discover just how strong and beautiful they really are

Contents

· ·

Introduction

Three years ago I wrote *Just Hand Over the Chocolate and No One Will Get Hurt*. The response has been phenomenal—I get the most amazing e-mails and letters from women all over the world. They are coping with stress and PMS, surviving cancer and divorce and depression. They tell me about their husbands, their kids and grandkids, their parents and their best friends. One woman sent me a poem her husband had written her (the handwritten original, no less!). Another woman sent photos of her kids. I get recipes and bookmarks. I even received a great "stress-busting kit" that contained a kazoo, liquid bubbles—and a crowbar!

I've had women identify with my practice of carrying tweezers in my car and plucking chin hairs at stoplights. Other women share my militant passion for chocolate, like the woman I met at a book signing who leaned in close and hissed, "Never, never, *never* eat chocolate with nuts—the nuts take up valuable space!"

But what really moves me are the notes that say, "Until I read your book, I felt so alone. I thought I was the only woman . . ."

Of course, at that point the phrases differ. One woman might finish the sentence by writing ". . . suffering from depression," while another might say ". . . going crazy from stress," while yet another might admit "... who has thrown away a perfectly good lunch box rather than face the advancing life-forms that have been allowed to breed in it over spring break."

I cried over the letter from a woman who shared that, on the night she was told that the lump in her breast was malignant, she followed a suggestion from one of my chapters and sang TV-land theme songs with her husband until her panic subsided and she was finally able to fall asleep.

We all share the human condition: stress, crisis, depression, emotional pain, heartache, triumph, dreams, and desires. No one is immune. In fact, the way I figure it, even Diane Sawyer gets morning breath and Vanna White knows how to spell flatulence.

Know what else we have in common?

How about the desire to experience greater joy, passion, purpose, and healing in our lives? (Which, of course, happens to be exactly what this book is about.)

Wow! you might be saying. Are there really things we can do and choices we can make that have the power to do all that? When we're feeling wounded or overwhelmed by life, can we find ways to heal, to hope, to live fully, and even to laugh again? It's a tall order, I know. And yet, when life has made us grumpy, nothing less will do.

(Sigh.) As always, much of this book has been born of my own experiences. I wish I could say it wasn't so. But the fact is, the past couple years have been some of the most difficult of my life as challenges in my life and marriage have spurred me to forge new trails in my own journey.

In the following pages, I'll share some of my own struggles. I'll also talk about the experiences of women I know. Better yet, I'll tell you about the paths we walked that eventually led to places of healing, hope, passion, and joy.

And let's not forget the magic ingredient. Because even though we may be touching on some serious subjects, we're going to share plenty of laughter as well! So join me as we discover:

- how to ask for what we need out of life
- how we can feel vibrantly alive by taking a few risks now and then
- how we can "think" our way to stronger, healthier, sexier bodies
- the little-known truth about secrets
- four ways to evict emotional pain
- why borrowing problems from our friends can improve our lives
- how to belly dance our way to emotional wellness

. . . and much, much more!

If I were to sum up my last book in one phrase, it would be this: When you find yourself in emotional crisis of any kind—stress, depression, PMS—here are fourteen ways to feel better.

The book you're holding in your hands says: And here's fourteen more.

You'll find the same blend of humor and help, the same marriage of comedy and common sense, the same diversity of suggestions, ranging from quick fixes to soul solutions.

You'll also find reflected in these pages a community of sorts, a sisterhood of women, a circle of friends. The fact that we may never have crossed paths doesn't mean that we don't share deep bonds of common experiences or haven't enriched each other's lives with hard-won insights.

And the truth is that the person who is getting the lion's share of the blessings is me. I feel that each woman who reads something I've written—not to mention the hundreds who have written me back—enriches my life in a profound manner. Being able to laugh, cry, and brainstorm together through letters, e-mail, and the pages of these books is a joy and a privilege that I don't take lightly.

Have you ever been in emotional pain or crisis? Has life ever made you grumpy? Have you ever suspected that your bed is the only bed in town with *two* wrong sides?

Then come on in and pull up a chair, because you've come to the right spot. When life hurts, what helps? We're going to figure it out together.

Just you and me and several thousand of our closest friends.

1

....

Just between Friends

I don't know about you, but I for one had all these amazing ideas growing up.

I thought that my life was going to be simple and perfect, just one Kodak moment after another.

I figured I would keep house like Donna Reed, raise my kids like Harriet Nelson, and wear the same dress size as Jane Wyatt.

I used to think life was going to be a bed of roses . . . a piece of cake . . . a walk in the park. Of course, what I didn't figure on, way back then, was that roses have thorns, cakes have calories, and a walk in the park increases your odds of stepping in doggie doo-doo.

Now wouldn't it be nice if I were the only woman on the face of the earth who had been surprised by the fact that life has turned out differently than she expected? Wouldn't it be great if I were the only woman since Eve who had experienced a gap, a rift, a chasm between happily-ever-after dreams and desires . . . and reality?

But my guess is that you know what it feels like to have life fall short of your expectations and end up filled with more stress or crisis or pain than you had originally planned!

It's enough to make you grumpy, isn't it?

Maybe you can relate with a few of my disillusionments with life:

I was naïve enough to believe my husband when he said it would eventually be my turn to hold the TV remote.

I thought "self-cleaning" ovens actually cleaned themselves. (Actually, I was kind of hoping that, if I asked nicely, mine might even do a couple loads of laundry at the same time.)

I figured women were just making up that stuff about men always forgetting to put the toilet seat back down.

I just assumed my kids would be close in age, like my sisters and I were; I certainly never expected to find myself shopping for a training bra and a diaper pail on the same trip to Target.

I thought when they said "one size fits all," they meant it.

I believed "happily ever after" was some sort of unwritten guarantee, like death and taxes. Phrases like "stress management" or "emotional pain" or "depression" simply were not supposed to be part of my vocabulary.

Fairy Tales

I don't know about you, but I used to think I was the only woman in the world who wasn't living a fairy-tale life. I actually bought into all the picture-perfect facades and masks that people wore around me.

Now I know better.

Even the Bible tells us that there's nothing new under the sun, no problem we face that isn't common to humankind.

We're all in the same boat, ladies.

In fact, let me tell you about three friends of mine. Like you and me, they've learned a few things about life. Among other things, they've learned that life isn't always a bed of roses . . . that the human spirit is far more resilient than any of us ever wanted to experience firsthand . . . and that the phrase "And they lived happily ever after" is actually a long-forgotten medieval punchline that, translated, means, "And, boy—ha ha!—are they in for the surprise of their lives!"

These friends look picture-perfect on the outside. But they know as well as anyone else that life is filled with ups and downs, cheers and tears, triumph and tragedy.

I'm talking about three women we know and love. Their names? Cinderella, Snow White, and Rapunzel.

Don't look so surprised. Sure, you and I remember the regal settings. We remember the handsome princes who saved the day. We remember how the kiss of true love changed everything. We remember the magic and the romance and the happy endings.

And yet . . .

Cinderella came from a family so dysfunctional, they'd make guests on the Jerry Springer show seem like the Waltons in comparison.

Snow White lived with a man dubbed "Grumpy" by those who knew him best.

And Rapunzel *couldn't* have had a very good sex life! I'm guessing that, after letting her two-hundred-pound lover hang from her tresses as he scaled the tower wall, she wasn't kidding when she shook her head and said, "Not tonight, dear, I have a headache."

My point is, not even the fairy-tale Queens lived fairy-tale lives. Bottom line, these gals had problems, too.

You don't believe me? Just think about the adjustments they had to make living with their handsome heroes. Can't you just hear these women a few months after the honeymoon?

"Why can't you ever put your socks in the hamper? Who do you think you are, royalty or something?"

"What do you mean just because I didn't give you a son you get to have sex with our nubile young chambermaid?"

"If you think I'm going to stand by while you marry our adolescent daughter off to the eighty-seven-year-old king of Brumania just so you get access to half his fleet, well, you'd better think again, buster!"

Whether our address is Anytown, USA, or page sixty-seven of *Tales from the Brothers Grimm*, when daily stresses, unmet expectations, and broken dreams leave us feeling bruised and wounded, life doesn't feel like a fairy tale, does it?

So what do we do about it? How can we cope? When we're stressed or hurting, can we find healthy ways to rediscover joy? In our relationships with our men, parents, friends, and children, can we learn to laugh and love without losing ourselves in the process? Can we seize the best and forgive the rest?

The truth is, life is filled with bedlam and blessings. It is both blemished and beautiful.

Can we find the inner strength to embrace it all?

Cappuccino Confessions

Not long ago, several friends and I decided we were overdue for a "Girls' Night Out." We had a great time eating Mexican food, going to a movie, and then chatting in a coffeehouse over mocha cappuccinos.

We found ourselves talking about the days we wake up grumpy (and about the days *that* particular honor belongs to our husbands or kids!). We talked about life in general and emotional crises in particular. And among the four of us, we pretty much covered it all: daily stresses, broken dreams, unexpected disappointments, and unforgiven hurts.

All too soon, the coffeehouse lights flickered off and back on, and we realized we were the last customers in the small cafe. The college student running the place turned the key in the front door, then nodded to us on her way back toward the kitchen. "Don't rush," she said. "You're welcome to stay till I'm done cleaning up." We accepted her generous offer, lingering another forty-five minutes over cold coffee and intimate confessions.

The conversation shifted as we went from sharing problems to pondering solutions. We talked about how each one of us might not only escape the chains of stress, disappointments, and past hurts but go on to . . .

experience true healing,

entertain new hope,

encounter fresh passion, and

embrace vibrant joy.

You and I may not be able to chat over cappuccinos, but we *can* enjoy some encouraging girltalk through the pages of this book. I've always said that when girlfriends get together, it's time well spent if they've managed to laugh, cry, and eat chocolate.

I'll take care of the laughter and the tears.

You bring the chocolate.

2

Take a Chance

My husband, Larry, loves adventure. Last year he went on a five-day hiking excursion.

In Peru.

I know this sounds amazing, but Larry flew to Peru for the sole purpose of hiking the Inca Trail.

The trip accomplished a lot. For one thing, if Larry is ever a contestant on a game show and is asked, for a grand prize of several million dollars, "Have you ever flown to Peru for the sole purpose of hiking the Inca Trail?" he's going to be a very wealthy man.

The trip accomplished something else as well. It pushed Larry to his physical limit and beyond. And that's not surprising. The Inca Trail is a grueling twenty-five-mile ordeal at nose-bleed altitudes. At nearly fourteen thousand feet above sea level, the air is so thin that spit has the density of a brick—a well-placed loogie will kill a man. Indeed, at one point during his oxygen-sparse trek, my typically frugal husband felt so fatigued that he considered chucking his brand-new $300 all-weather backpacking tent just to lighten his load.

By the time Larry found himself back on American soil, he not only felt more alive, he was thrilled just to *be* alive.

Risk can have that effect on a person.

If you're not convinced that taking a risk can make you feel more alive, just ask a kid. Kids know all about risks.

Recently my fourteen-year-old daughter, Kaitlyn, hosted a slumber party for her friends and, quite frankly, the evening was riddled with risks. The girls began by calling boys they liked and giggling anonymously into the phone. (I suppose I should have stopped them. I might have, too, if that kind of irresponsible and annoying behavior didn't hold such a cherished place in my own bank of adolescent memories.) Next on the agenda? A dozen rounds of truth-or-dare and then, at midnight, toilet-papering the house of a friend. (I have to admit I was an accessory to the crime—I drove the getaway car.)

It was an exhilarating evening. And no wonder, because whether we're talking about hiking twenty miles, papering a house, making an intimate confession, or calling a heartthrob (whose mother may or may not subscribe to caller I.D.), there's nothing quite as invigorating as taking a calculated risk.

I wish I had a few risk-taking stories of my own, but I live a pretty tame life. In fact, my life is so tame that in order to have anything worthwhile to say in this chapter, I figured I should go out and do something really wild just to write about it. (Bungee jumping came to mind, but about that time my doctor changed my medication and I haven't considered it since.)

But then it dawned on me that I didn't need to add any artificial spice to my life. The truth is, I take risks every day. My life brims with risk.

Danger is my middle name.

For example, I take my life in my hands every time I open the vegetable bin of my refrigerator. Have you ever had to dispose of a plastic bag containing cucumbers that time has reduced to little more than toxic brown soup and spongy mounds of mold? If not, count yourself lucky. Not every woman who has done so has lived to tell the story.

I also take my life in my hands every time I get in my van. This is because the passenger window doesn't unroll, the air conditioner only works in arctic-blast mode, the engine overheats every three days, and if you leave the sliding door open for more than a few minutes, the overhead light drains the battery, and you have to ask for a jump from strangers who may or may not be serial killers disguised as roadside angels.

And I definitely take my life in my hands every time I feed our dog. At fifty pounds, our white German shepherd, Walter, has reached half of his adult size. As it is, he gallops through the house like a Shetland pony on Metabolife. To make matters worse, when I took Walter to the vet last week, the kindly doctor looked at my dog and said, "Is he a wolf hybrid?"

"Excuse me?" I said. "Part wolf? I don't think so. Why?"

"Some of them are, you know. He's got a few of the bodily characteristics. But he doesn't have the eyes. So he might not be," he said nonchalantly as he went back to the exam.

"Hold on," I sputtered. "I mean . . . if he was, you know, part wolf, what does that mean?"

The vet shrugged. "It means I'd watch him."

Oh great. Thank you very much. So now I'm living with a wolf the size of a Harley Davidson. And growing.

You know, that Inca Trail is starting to look like a piece of cake.

The Therapeutic Benefits of Risk

I guess I started thinking about risks because I'm always looking for new ways to invite more joy, passion, and purpose into my life, and risk-taking just seems like a natural way to do that. When we take a chance—in matters of the heart or life and limb—we feel incredibly alive, don't we? With the adrenaline and endorphins and whatever else gets thrown into the hormonal stew, we feel a heady rush. A slight intoxication. A giddy delight.

What a great feeling!

You know, a lot of days I wake up feeling anything *but* giddy and intoxicated with life. In fact—I hate to admit this—but on a lot of mornings I wake up kind of, you know . . .

Grumpy.

Some days I feel overworked, overwhelmed, and underappreciated. Disillusionment creeps into the mix now and then, as does depression. Other days my life feels incredibly calculated. Measured. Predictable. Still other days it's not the tedium of life that gets me down but the tenacity of the hurts I've accumulated along the way. Whether it's an old wound that just won't heal or a current relationship that is causing me pain, some days my heart hurts with an ache that Advil just can't touch.

My guess is that none of this is news to you. My guess is that you know what it feels like to look at your life and find, at the address where passion, purpose, and joy used to reside, little more than an empty mailbox. A neglected yard. Dark windows. And you wonder where those old friends have gone and how you can get them to come home.

Now obviously risk-taking isn't the only solution. That's why, in the following pages, you'll find not just one but fourteen ideas to help you experience greater passion, purpose, and joy in your life.

But risk-taking isn't a bad place to start. This is because when I'm feeling grumpy or numb or disillusioned, one of the things that can get me jump-started is that invigorating rush I feel when I step outside the box, when I cross the white picket fence that signals the end of my comfort zone.

You Win Some . . .

So what kind of risks am I talking about? You're the best judge of what constitutes risk to you. To me, public speaking is a piece of cake, while getting some folks behind a podium can require a handful of Valium and a cattle prod. You, on the other hand, might be able to balance your checkbook in your sleep, while I break out in hives and require therapy at the very thought.

I asked friends of mine to tell me about risks they've taken in the past twelve months. I asked them to describe something they chose to do that was just a little beyond their comfort zone.

For Nancy Rottmeyer, taking a risk meant volunteering to teach a Sunday school class for four- and five-year-olds. She says, "When I think of risk, I tend to think of parachuting or something like that. But teaching this class was a real risk for me because it meant overcoming not just a fear of failure but also this nagging fear that other people were better equipped for the job, and I shouldn't even be giving it a try."

For years Dana Smith worked for major organizations as a writer, but her dream had always been to launch a freelance career and work from home. When her husband received a promotion at work, Dana saw the chance to try to make her dream come true. She took a risk and quit her full-time job and began submitting query letters to magazines. Even if Dana had never landed a freelance assignment, she could have held her head high, knowing that her willingness to take a risk was an accomplishment in itself. But Dana did land an assignment. And then another. And another. One year later, she says taking the leap was a great move and she's thrilled with the results.

My friend Darrell Purdy has been disfigured from birth. Embarrassed by the shape of his mouth, chin, hands, and feet, Darrell had never pursued a romantic relationship with a woman. He is one of the most intelligent and sensitive men I know, but he had never had a girlfriend. All that changed when a friendship with a colleague sparked into something more. Falling in love was the most frightening and exhilarating experience of his life. Darrell had waited forty years for the chance to love someone. If the relationship crashed and burned could he survive the blow? He wasn't sure. All he knew was that he was willing to take the risk.

Sometimes you just gotta take a leap.

You Lose Some…

I took a chance recently, but the outcome was much different than I had imagined. I logged on to the Internet and invested a few thousand dollars in a sure-thing company. The stock I bought at fifty bucks a share has dropped considerably. At this point, a couple shares of this stock and three bucks would buy me a Frappuccino.

That can happen, you know. A relationship-shy woman can take a chance on a blind date—and find herself spending three hours with a man who makes her wish she were somewhere else. Anywhere else. Like getting a root canal or being audited by the IRS.

The grandmother who trains for the Boston Marathon might sprain her ankle five miles into the race and find herself observing the finish line on her motel room TV.

So what do you do when you take a risk and it doesn't pay off like you hoped?

Nuggets of Gold

I wish I had a nice little cliché that would numb the pain of taking a leap . . . and ending up in a crumpled heap as a result.

But I don't. It hurts.

All I can say is this: You know that fiery, consuming pain? Eventually it begins to subside a little. And then a lot. And when you stir the ashes where the pain once flared, you find little pieces of gold. Hard, bright nuggets glittering in the black ash. Character. Insights. Wisdom. Empathy. Strength. Look deeper still and you'll discover a new dream, hiding there in the soot. A new ideal or goal that's worthy of risk. A different vision. Another hope.

I believe this. I really do. I believe that in order to really live, we've got to be willing to take some risks, riding the wave of pain or ecstasy that follows.

Nancy's success as a Sunday school teacher is evidenced by the ready hugs of the kids who adore her. Dana's freelance career is thriving. I lost money in the stock market.

As for Darrell, he and Haley broke up. As I write this, Darrell is in crisis; but every day he's stronger and a little more hopeful about his life. He's hurting, no doubt about that. But he's going to be all right.

Even witnessing my friend in great pain, I believe his decision to take chance on love was the right one.

We can live safe and avoid pain. Or we can embrace risk, laughing well and crying hard and living big.

Want to feel alive? Enrich your world? Experience greater passion? Risk-taking isn't always the answer. Sometimes we need to pay attention to the intuitive voice deep in our belly saying, "Don't." Other times we need to seek out a safe place in which we can hunker down and ride out life's storms. And sometimes—and these are enviable times indeed—the wind is right and there's a scent of adventure in the air, and we'd do well to pack some bug repellent and granola bars and strike out for the horizon.

And if the thought of all that risk and adventure still makes you queasy, just call me. I'll be happy to let you borrow Walter. He's really good company, he can bark at strangers, and the hairs he'll shed all over your clothing can serve as an extra layer to help keep you warm at night.

Not to mention the fact that, if you get tired on your journey, you can always saddle up and ride him.

3

....

Speak Up, Dearie

I t was seven o'clock on a Sunday evening. My friend Belinda Bai and I were piddling around in my kitchen, where I had just spent the last twenty minutes bragging to her about the best chocolate chip cookie recipe in the world.

"So go to Sam's Club and buy the industrial-sized bag of Ghirardelli's milk chocolate chips," I concluded. "The recipe is on the back of the bag. In fact . . ." I got a happy gleam in my eyes. "I've talked about it so much that we've just GOT to make some this very minute!"

I went to the cupboard and pulled out a huge Tupperware container filled with Ghirardelli's milk chocolate chips. Cracking the lid, I reached in and drew out a piece of plastic I had snipped from the back of the bag that the chocolate chips came in.

Now let me say here that organization is not my specialty. I doubt that I have an organized bone in my body. In fact, last time I checked, my thigh bone not only was NOT connected to my knee bone, it had been misplaced entirely and hadn't been seen in a week. So I was pretty pleased with myself that I'd had the foresight to save the recipe from the back of the wrapper.

I waved it now. "In fact, I've got the recipe right here!"

I looked at the piece of plastic in my hand and groaned. I was holding a list of nutritional values of milk chocolate chips.

Apparently I'd been so intoxicated by my frenzy of organization that I'd saved the wrong piece of wrapper.

Belinda said, "What a shame. Those cookies were really sounding good."

I said, "I'm calling Sam's."

"Who?"

"I'm calling Sam's Club."

"You can't call the store. It's Sunday night. They're closed."

"Maybe. We'll see. Tonight it's Ghirardelli's or bust."

I dialed. The phone rang. A man answered. My hope soared until he informed me he was the night guard. Sam's was closed after all.

But it was Ghirardelli's cookies or die.

I carefully explained that one of my friends and I were about to expire a slow, painful death from lack of Ghirardelli's chocolate chip cookies and that I'd been disorganized since childhood, but that I'd had this one shining moment of organization, except I'd thrown away the recipe after all, and now we were desperate, and could he *pleasepleaseplease* help us out?

The man sounded puzzled as he said, "I'm just the security guy. I don't understand how you think I can help."

I enlightened him. "I need you to walk to the chocolate chip aisle, grab a bag of Ghirardelli's, bring it back to the phone, and read me the recipe off the back of the bag."

So he did.

Belinda and I got our chocolate fix after all.

We also got a nice lesson in the art of negotiation: Sometimes it pays to ask for what you want.

Would You Like a Coronary with Your Coffee?

I have lots of stories about negotiating the strangest things with total strangers. But perhaps my favorite story is the time we nearly put my father-in-law in the hospital.

It all started when Dad, a college professor and adminis-
trator at Anderson University for more than thirty-five years,
wrote us about a retirement dinner the university was hosting
in his honor. Dad also wrote, "But don't come. It's too much
money to fly from Texas to Indiana, and I want to spare you
the time and expense."

Larry decided to surprise his father by showing up unan-
nounced for the special event.

Suddenly I had an idea. I asked Larry, "Want to REALLY
surprise your dad?"

Larry said, "How?"

"Does your dad still eat breakfast at Hardee's every Saturday morning?" Hardee's is a fast food joint, sort of like
McDonald's or Burger King.

Larry thought a minute. "I think so. Why?"

I said, "Trust me."

I got on the phone, called Hardee's, and made all the ar-
rangements. Using my best negotiating tactics, I somehow
talked the manager into letting Larry slip into a Hardee's uni-
form and wait behind the counter for Dad to show up for
breakfast.

Larry flew into town on a Friday night and stayed with a
friend. On Saturday morning he "went to work" at Hardee's.
At precisely nine o'clock, my mother-in-law, father-in-law,
and cousins Forry and Zula Carlson entered Hardee's. The
three fellow conspirators sent Dad to the counter to order,
then hung back to watch the fun.

Larry, wearing the Hardee's shirt and hat, stepped up to the
counter and faced his dad. He said, "Your order, please."

Dad looked at him.

There was a long pause.

Everyone held their breath.

Dad said, "I'll have the breakfast burrito."

Larry said, "We're out of those."

Dad said, "In that case, I guess I'll have a sausage biscuit."

Larry said, "We're out of those, too."

Dad said, "I've never heard of such a thing! Well then, just give me a cup of coffee."

Larry said, "We're out of coffee, too."

Dad's face and neck began to flush. "How can you be out of coffee? I can see the coffeepot right behind you!"

At about that time, Larry took off his paper cap and burst into laughter. "Hey, Dad, don't you recognize your own son?"

I wasn't there at the time. But I understand that what happened next was like a scene straight out of that old sitcom *Sanford and Son,* where Fred Sanford grabs his heart and staggers backwards, claiming to be heaven-bound.

'Cept Dad wasn't faking.

He didn't have a heart attack. But he staggered backwards in shock. Good thing family members were there to catch him. I probably should have negotiated some paramedics into the deal as well. My father-in-law lived to attend his retirement dinner that night, and to this day loves to tell the story of Larry's twelve-minute career as a clerk at Hardee's.

I used to think that negotiating was mainly for business executives. Now I know it's the stuff of life. Whether we're negotiating emotional boundaries, paychecks, curfews, chores, or deadlines—not to mention cookie recipes and practical jokes—it certainly doesn't hurt to know how to ask for what we want and need.

Read My Mind

I don't know about you, but I have a hard time asking for what I want and need out of life.

Oh, not with total strangers. I can ask a total stranger to dictate a cookie recipe, but when it comes to the real relationships in my life—relationships with folks who are in my life on a daily basis—I tend to take a different approach.

Like with Larry. I can't begin to tell you all the times I've expected him to read my mind. For a number of years, when it came to sex, birthday presents, compliments, housework, and more, I just expected him to be in the know. I even expected him to magically know *when* I was upset, and more importantly, *why* I was upset.

But the man would make a horrible fortune-teller. Not only does he look awful in bangles, he's clueless when it comes to discerning the unspoken. I mean, we've actually had conversations where he says to me, "Are you mad at me?" and I say, "no," AND HE BELIEVES ME! WHAT CAN HE POSSIBLY BE THINKING!!!

So sometimes I don't talk about my wants and needs because I apparently prefer extrasensory perception to English.

Perhaps, like me, you're stressed out or in emotional pain, but you don't ask people around you for what you need because somehow you believe it will "mean more" if they figure it out on their own.

Can you and I begin to see how illogical that is?

I get on my kids about this all the time. Recently I found Kacie sitting by herself in the living room. She was in tears. I hurried to her side and asked her what had happened.

Through sobs, she managed to heave out the words, "At lunchtime you didn't give me anything to drink with my sandwich."

"Did you *ask* for something to drink? Did you say, 'Hey, you forgot my juice! Mom, could I have some juice, please?' Did you say that?"

She shook her head.

"If you want something, Kacie, you have to say it. With your *mouth*. Now let's practice. Say, 'Mom, I need some juice, please.' Can you say it?"

"Mom, I need some juice, please."

"I would *love* to get you some juice, Kacie. Come on. Let's go to the kitchen."

I'm trying to teach my kids that while my swami turban is at the cleaners, they'll just have to go through the extra effort of forming their mouths around actual words.

Who knows? Maybe one day I'll manage to master that lesson myself. And just in case you struggle with the same thing, as soon as I figure it all out I'll send you a message and let you know how I did it.

Hopefully you'll hear from me soon.

Check your thoughts daily.

Martyr Mom Strikes Again

One of the reasons I hesitate to articulate my needs is because of the whole mind-reading thing.

A second reason is because somewhere in my head lives a two-inch Martyr Mom, wearing a garage-sale dress and a five-dollar haircut, who frequently reminds me that nice girls and good wives and mothers are supposed to do without.

Maybe you've met her. In fact, it's possible that you have one of her relatives living in your head. If so, she may have said these kinds of things to you over the years:

"I know you're feeling stressed, but you can't go away for that weekend with your husband. . . . What kind of mother leaves her kids with a babysitter for two whole days?"

"Sure, you'd love to get in shape. But an exercise program takes too much time. Your family would suffer!"

"You only *wish* you were worth more money at the office. Yes, yes, I know you're working harder than your colleagues, but you really shouldn't ask for a raise because you're really not worth it."

"I agree that it was unrealistic for your sister to ask you to host the family July 4th weekend at your house—with less than a week's notice! But you shouldn't ask her to help you with the cooking—if you were a good enough homemaker you could handle this on your own."

"I realize your friends keep pestering you to sign up for the church women's retreat, but it would mean asking your husband to postpone his fishing trip till the following weekend, and you certainly can't do THAT!"

"Your daughter doesn't want to put her new baby in daycare and wants you to watch him instead. I know you feel panicked at the thought, but you just can't say no. As a good mom and grandmother, you really should be willing to drop everything in your life for the sake of your loved ones. Your needs will just have to come last!"

I love to take care of other people. I really do. I love hosting parties and nurturing my kids and helping the elderly and giving encouragement to friends my age. I love being able to say, "Yes!" when someone I love approaches me and says, "Could you . . ."

But if Martyr Mom had her diabolical way, there's one person I would never serve. One person whose needs would always come last. And that person would be me.

Funny thing though: While Martyr Mom always seems to be around to remind me to neglect myself, she's never around to help me pick up the pieces when my self-neglect turns ugly. When I explode in resentment at my husband, when I dissolve into tears of stress, when I give in to depression, Martyr Mom simply can't be found.

I've looked for her during those times, just so I could say to her, "If only I had replenished my spirit by taking care of my own needs now and then, I'd be much happier right now and so would my family!"

But the windows of her tiny house are dark, there are newspapers piled in the front yard, and there's a note on her door. It says, "Be back soon. Gone to the Bahamas."

Apparently even Martyr Mom needs to look after herself now and then.

Asking for What You Need? It's As Easy As ABC!

Are you overworked? Stressed-out? In emotional pain? Feeling grumpy?

Then let me ask you one more question: Is there something that you need that you're not asking for?

Perhaps you need more help around the house, or a quiet night with your husband, or distance from a toxic relationship. Perhaps you need more respectful communication from your kids. Maybe you need to give yourself permission to say no to overcommitment. It's possible you need to tell your husband that you want to seek professional help and you'd like for him to come with you. Perhaps you need more downtime with your friends, or you want to join a women's Bible study at your church. It's possible your family doesn't go to church and you feel spiritually parched, so you need to find spiritual fellowship where you can be refreshed. Maybe your soul is thriving, but your body is a mess, and what you really need is an hour a day to walk, pump iron, swim, jog, or kickbox your way to a healthier you—or maybe just a good pedicure!

Can you ask for what you want and need?

Sometimes it helps to have the cooperation of friends and family members. But sometimes the person who is denying you what you need is the same woman who stares back at you every morning from the bathroom mirror.

One woman told me, "I was 150 pounds overweight and having problems with my circulation. My kids said, 'Get out and walk!' My husband said, 'Get out and walk!' I'm the one who wouldn't give myself permission to leave my family for an hour at a time and do something good for me."

Whether you are negotiating with friends and family or negotiating with yourself, here are seven suggestions that will help you ask for the things you need so you can experience the best that life has to offer.

Articulate What You Want

My daughter Kaitlyn is a very articulate fourteen-year-old. But I shouldn't be surprised; she's been articulate for years.

When she was less than two years old, she developed the morning ritual of climbing out of her crib, toddling to my bedroom in her little footie pajamas, standing at the side of the bed, and patting my arm until I was awake. Then once she had my bleary-eyed attention, this is what she said in very precisely enunciated words: "I want something to eat, and something to drink, and cartoons on TV." Those exact words. Every single morning. For months. She knew exactly what she wanted, and she asked for it.

Do you know what you want and need that will encourage healing, joy, and passion in your life?

Decide what you need. Then put it into words. Not sure how? Try this simple formula:

"I want _____." (fill in the blank)

Or "I need _____." (fill in the blank)

Broaden Your Perspective

It's easy, when negotiating, to focus on the problem you are trying to solve in *your* life. But for your best shot at success, think about the person with whom you're negotiating. What are his or her needs and desires? If you can solve one of the other person's problems while getting your own needs met, you have created a truly win-win situation.

My friend Beth faced an unusual problem a couple years ago. She was friends with Julie, a neighbor who lived next door. Beth's friendship with Julie was enjoyable except for one flaw: Julie not only wanted to get together every day for lunch, shopping, or chatting, she wanted to spend holidays together and even suggested fencing the two yards into one large compound.

Beth says, "She was smothering me. I didn't have time for the kind of intense friendship she wanted, and I desperately needed some space! But I knew Julie was lonely, and I didn't want to hurt her feelings. I didn't know what to do!"

Beth identified her own need: She needed space. She decided she would enjoy socializing with Julie twice a week. Then she identified Julie's need: Julie needed to feel accepted and affirmed. Beth knew it meant a lot to Julie when she called and initiated lunch or a movie.

Finally, she devised a solution that solved both dilemmas. Each week, she accepted only one of Julie's invitations, turning down the rest by explaining that she had other commitments. But sometime during that same week, Beth would invite Julie over for coffee or out shopping.

Their friendship has survived and thrived. Beth received the space she needed while giving Julie the affirmation *she* needed.

Neophyte negotiators ask the question, "How can you help me meet my needs?" But the best negotiators broaden their perspective. They ask the question, "What do you need, and how can I help you achieve your goal while getting my needs met in the process?"

Choose Your Words Carefully

If you want your loved ones to take your request seriously, stop apologizing for having needs! Avoid phrases like: "I know you're going to say no, but I wanted to ask anyway. . . ."

Or "I'll understand if you can't do what I'm about to ask. . . ."

Or "I know I'm being pushy, but . . ."

These phrases make it nearly impossible for your request to receive the careful consideration that it deserves!

Don't Fidget

Are you in the process of asking for something you need? Here's a simple tip: Don't fidget. Watch your body language.

Don't hem and haw either. Just take a deep breath and spit it out. Go back to the "formula" I mentioned before. Say, "I need . . ." or "I want . . ." and fill in the blank. Practice saying the words out loud, by yourself. Get your mouth used to the shape and taste of the words so that when you need to say them for real, you can say them with conviction and finesse.

If Words Could Kill . . .

The following phrases can spell death to your negotiations. Don't sabotage your request before it even leaves your mouth. When you can, steer clear of the following phrases:

"I know you're going to say 'no,' but . . ."
"I know this is a horrible thing to ask, but would you mind terribly if . . ."
"You're not going to like this, but . . ."
"I'm really sorry; I hate to ask this, but . . ."
"Now don't feel bad about saying no to what I'm about to ask. . . ."
"I hate to be pushy, but . . ."

Here are a handful of healthier choices when it comes to phrasing your request:

"My needs are . . ."
"To make this a win-win situation, we could . . ."
"My goal is . . ."
"I've thought about this, and I've decided that what I'm going to need is . . ."

Entertain Lots of Options

Whether you are negotiating with your family or with yourself, try this approach. At the top of a piece of paper, write down a need in your life. For example, you might write, "I'm lonely, and I need to cultivate more contact with other people." On the rest of the paper, write ways to meet that need. Write as many solutions as you can think of. They may range from "Get a pen pal" to "Join a dating service" to "Start attending church."

When you're trying to meet a need or solve a problem, don't just come up with Plan A—come up with Plans B through Z as well. The more the merrier! Then choose the one that works best for everyone involved.

Frame Your Request as a Favor

Sometimes this works wonders. Everyone likes the good feeling that comes from helping another person. Some examples:

"I need a favor. . . . Could you watch the kids Tuesday night while I go to class?"

"I'm overcommitted, and I really need to create some space in my life. It would help me tremendously if you could fill in for me on Saturday."

"I can't believe I lost that Ghirardelli chocolate chip cookie recipe! You'd be doing me a tremendous service if you could read it to me over the phone!"

"You don't know me, but I have a favor to ask. My husband would like to surprise his dad, and we need your help with a practical joke."

You get the idea!

Give a Little

Negotiations are about give-and-take. Know what you're willing to give.

Sometimes I negotiate with my kids about going to sleep at night. When Kaitlyn—who happens to think bedtime falls into the category of "cruel and unusual punishment"—was about three or four, she posed a particular challenge. As soon as she got horizontal, she'd flail and writhe like a worm on a hook. No wonder the sandman took so long in coming—he knew he'd risk a black eye if he got too close.

Knowing my tired preschooler would fall right to sleep if she could lie still for even a moment, I began my negotiations like this: "Kaitlyn, I have a deal for you. If you lie perfectly still and close your eyes and *pretend* to be asleep for, oh, say, six hours, I'll let you get up and play."

"I don't have to *really* go to sleep? Just pretend?"

"Just pretend. Just lie still and close your eyes. You never have to actually go to sleep."

My shrewd daughter would say, "Six hours is too long. How about three?"

"Five hours is as low as I'm willing to go."

"Make it four and you've got a deal."

I'd give a heavy sigh. "Ohhhh, alright. You're a good negotiator, Kaitlyn."

She'd be asleep in thirty seconds.

This works. Really. Just don't try it with kids who can tell time.

Give-and-take. You don't always have to begin with your final offer. Know what's negotiable and what's not, and allow yourself a margin to get the most from your bargaining.

So here they are again, negotiating tips as easy as ABC:

Articulate what you want

Broaden your perspective

Choose your words carefully

Don't fidget

Entertain lots of options

Frame your request as a favor

Give a little.

Who knows? Maybe in heaven all we'll have to do is think a thought to have it come true.

But here on earth, we'd better learn how to articulate our needs the old-fashioned way. We won't always get what we want, but any way we look at it, being honest and up front about legitimate needs is the best strategy for healthy living.

It's also the best way I know to get outrageous favors from total strangers.

Cookie, anyone?

4

Name It, Tame It

My six-year-old has a funny history with names. When she was first learning to talk, Kacie easily mastered words like "dog" and "apple" and "tea" (she's our native Texan, after all).

The word that she refused to say was "Daddy."

But it's not like she didn't have a name for him. She did. She called him "Mom."

Every night when she heard his key in the front door, she would drop whatever she was doing and race through the house, her arms outstretched in anticipation of a hug, her face glowing, all the while happily calling his name: "Mom! Mom!"

We tried everything we could think of to help her broaden her vocabulary, to no avail. Driving in the car, we would coach her. "Look, Kacie, this is DAD. Can you say DAD?" Sitting at the dinner table, we would quiz her. "Kacie, where's Mama? That's right! Now where's your sister? Good job! Now where is Daddy? Kacie? Can you point to Daddy? Which one is Daddy? Hello? Kacie? Are you listening?"

Every time she called him "Mom," Larry gently corrected her and even threw in a bribe now and then. "I'm not Mom, I'm Dad. Can you say Dad? Please? Just say Dad. Say Dad and

I'll buy you a new Fisher-Price tricycle. A new dolly. Season tickets for the Cowboys. A candy-apple-red Porsche. Anything!"

Then one night, everything changed. The battle finally came to an end.

Larry was sitting cross-legged on the floor in our bedroom, his tool box at hand, assembling a Sit-Up Master. (You've probably seen the advertisements: "Flat Abs in Seven Minutes a Day! You'll Never Even Break into a Sweat! No Pain, All Gain! Look Like Cindy Crawford by Christmas! Buy Me! Buy Me Now!")

Yet I digress.

Larry was sitting cross-legged on the floor, sorting through nuts and bolts and pieces of pipe, when Kacie toddled over and plopped into his lap. She stayed there awhile, "helping" him with his task, while I lounged lazily on my stomach at the foot of our bed and watched the progress.

I hadn't moved a muscle in ten minutes when Larry, reaching for a tool, said nonchalantly, "Look, Kacie; Mom's working hard."

He's making fun of me! I thought, and I opened my mouth to object. But I never got the words out, because at that moment Larry went on to wave the Phillips in his hand and said, "See? This is a screwdriver, Kacie. Mom's using a screwdriver."

Suddenly I began to laugh.

Our battle was finally over. It ended the night Larry conceded, the night he threw in the towel and decided that a dad by any other name is still a dad.

Even if that name is "Mom."

The Name Game

Despite the fact that Kacie called Larry "Mom" and that for a long time her affectionate name for her sister happened to be "Doo-doo," I don't want you to think that we take names lightly around my house. In fact, as a rule, I work hard to help my kids come up with the right name for things.

I'll never forget the day I found Kacie on a chair in the kitchen. I looked at my daughter, then two and a half, and said matter-of-factly, "You've been eating the chocolate cake."

She stared at me wide-eyed, shook her white-blonde curls vigorously, and announced with no uncertainty, "No, I haven't been eating cake."

"No cake at all?" I said.

"No cake."

I sighed. "Kacie, let me help you out here. The truth is, you've been eating cake. But you keep telling me you haven't. This is called 'lying.' And it's not a wise choice. To help you remember not to tell lies, every time you tell one, you're going to have to spend some time in the time-out chair, starting right now."

She never did figure out how I knew she'd told a lie. Of course, an older child would have washed her face before denying the crime. I guess Kacie never dreamed that having chocolate frosting all over her face could actually give her away!

So we work at naming our behaviors. I'm always explaining things to her like, "This is called *lying*," or "This is called *stealing*." (Particularly after the time she walked out of a store with a Beanie Baby stuffed under her shirt. She tried to justify her action by saying that the toy was cold. That would be a hard sell any time of the year, but in Texas in July, it's tantamount to a full confession.)

We also work on naming emotions. When Kacie cried because one of her best friends had moved away, I helped her name the emotion: "Kacie, what you're feeling right now is called *grief*." When she was upset because she didn't get to accompany her sister on a school field trip, I said, "Kacie, you're feeling *disappointed*." When I became preoccupied with a deadline, Kacie responded by becoming whiney and clingy. Seeing that she was in crisis, I held her in my arms and gave

43

a name to the restless ache inside her. "Kacie, you're feeling *neglected,* and I don't blame you a bit."

When we give something a name—the right name—we gain some control over it. Name it, tame it, I say.

Emotional Pain

I'll never forget how relieved I felt the day my family doctor gave a title to something huge and menacing and nameless that I'd been wrestling with for several years.

I hadn't been able to put my finger on it. All I knew was that I couldn't concentrate, couldn't focus, couldn't sleep at night yet couldn't stay awake during the day. I spent hours sitting on the couch, watching the clock tick. I went days without brushing my teeth, combing my hair, or changing my clothes. I had no energy, no joy, no hope or purpose.

The doctor evaluated my symptoms, then said the three magic words that brought both terror and hope into my life: "You're clinically depressed."

Depression. Wow. What a scary word.

And yet . . .

By George, if it had a name, perhaps it had a cure. A wave of relief surged over my numb and exhausted spirit. It had a name. My enemy had a name. I felt the first stirrings of a fragile hope. Maybe I could lick this thing yet.

Depression and Denial

Names can be scary. Depression. Cancer. Addiction. Grief. Disillusionment. But what's the alternative? How can we effectively deal with something we aren't willing to name? It won't just go away if we ignore it.

Oh, there's plenty of stuff I'd love to ignore and hope that it just goes away on its own. I have a renegade tree growing up through the wooden planks of my back porch; I try to pretend the tree isn't there, but my denial hasn't stopped it from growing a little larger and stronger every day. Other topics of denial? How about my Visa bill, or the mysteriously bulging Tupperware in the back of my fridge?

You can see that I practice the art of denial in many areas of my life. One of these days my denial might actually make something unpleasant disappear from my life. (It's never happened yet, but a girl can dream, can't she?)

Until then, I guess there's no way around the truth: Denial doesn't work. In order to get rid of something unpleasant in our lives, we've usually got to face up to it first.

Naming my depression eight years ago was a critical first step toward taming it. What followed included two years of counseling, a season on antidepressants, and involvement with a caring church community where I built intimate friendships that helped me feel less isolated. All of this contributed to a wonderful healing that was ongoing for the next half-dozen years.

A couple years ago, however, I felt my old enemy grasping for territory that I had fought long and hard to reclaim. I began to feel numb and overwhelmed again. Focusing on even small tasks required a level of energy and concentration that I simply didn't have. I struggled for a year and managed to keep my depression at bay.

But just barely.

About that time, I began to face the fact that there remained a part of my life that had been causing me untold emotional pain for a very long time. Indeed, while I had worked hard to name and tame my depression, the truth is that Larry and I had not been particularly successful at naming and taming some foundational issues that were undermining our marriage—and fueling my depression. As a result of our joint denial, I had spent a lot of years trying to pretend that I wasn't hurting.

And my efforts were finally wearing thin.

One day I woke up, looked in the mirror, and took a good accounting of the toll of living with unnamed, untamed stress and pain for too long.

I was miserable. I was fighting to stay a step ahead of depression. I had gained 120 unwanted pounds. Somewhere along the way I had lost touch with my sense of femininity and sensuality. Larry and I were living like two strangers who just happened to share a mortgage and two kids. Even worse, I had given up any hope that my marriage and my life could be any different. Talk about feeling grumpy!

I heard a doctor once describe emotional pain like a beach ball. Imagine taking a large, inflated beach ball into the pool with you. Now, imagine yourself trying to keep it submerged at all times. Hard to do, isn't it? Oh, you can keep it under the surface for awhile, but it's a constant battle, and not infrequently the ball slips from your grasp and bobs unceremoniously to the surface. Emotional pain is just like that; it resists submersion and has the annoying tendency of bobbing to the surface when you least expect it.

I think the beach ball analogy is a good illustration. But if I were to paint a picture of emotional pain in my own words, from my own experience, I would describe emotional pain as an ocean.

When you live with unnamed, untamed emotional pain for a long time, it swells like an ocean inside of you. Over the years, while you're working overtime pretending it's not there, it's busy at work, lap, lap, lapping away at everything inside of you. And one morning you wake up and realize that the unrelenting waves of pain have managed to erode away not just your joy and your peace but your very boundaries. Suddenly you realize that you would do anything to stop the constant tides of pain that never seem to go away.

That was the scariest moment for me: to wake up and realize that the very parameters of who I was, what I was capable of, and where I would turn for relief had been detrimentally altered by my pain.

That's what denial will do to you.

You Have to Say "Hello" Before You Can Say "Good-bye"

I get the most amazing e-mails and letters from readers. Quite a few women have written to me, identifying with my story of clinical depression.

Often a woman will write something like this: "I've been struggling for several years, and reading your story was the first time I put a name to what was ailing me! Now that I realize I'm depressed, I've made an appointment to see a doctor and get help."

Clinical depression is just one example of something we might have to name before it can be tamed. What are some other examples of things we might have to face before we can experience true healing and freedom?

Here's what some other women have experienced in their lives:

Jennifer's marriage had limped along for years. It wasn't until she faced the fact that she and John were not only miserable but were creating a dysfunctional home life for their children that she drew a line in the sand. The couple sought counseling and got the help they needed to get their relationship back on track.

Sharon had good reason to feel stressed. Newly divorced with three young children, she often felt isolated and overwhelmed. One night after she put the kids to bed, she opened a bottle of champagne she kept on hand for company. The drink helped her relax and drift into sleep. Within a few months, she was drinking alone four or five evenings a week. When one of her girlfriends expressed concern, Sharon denied she had a drinking problem. It wasn't until her daughter woke up from a nightmare, cried alone for fifteen minutes, and then made her way downstairs to find Mommy drunk on the sofa, that Sharon finally faced the truth. She poured the alcohol down the drain and began looking for healthier ways to manage her stress and ease her isolation.

A married mom of two teenagers, Beth Ann worked in the office at her church. She felt herself drawn to Tony, an assistant pastor. Beth Ann remembers, "Tony and I talked about spiritual things, so I figured our relationship had to be okay. But before long we were looking for opportunities to be alone to kiss and hold each other. We still denied we were having an affair. Instead, we told ourselves we had a deep, spiritual relationship. We couldn't face reality, so we tried to dress it up as something acceptable."

When Beth Ann's husband, Steve, requested a job transfer to another state, she and Tony stayed in touch by phone and mail. It wasn't until her husband dragged her into counseling that the veneer of Beth Ann's denial began to crack.

"When I began to realize what I'd done, I thought I would fall apart," she says. "For the first time, I was seeing my dark side, and it felt overwhelming."

Beth Ann had been in denial for a long time, and as a result had traveled down a dangerous path. Embracing the truth was a pivotal first step to healing, although it didn't come overnight.

Months into counseling, Steve was still hurting. Every day he confronted his wife with the same angry question: "How could you have gotten caught up in an affair?"

One night Beth Ann shot back: "I've asked your forgiveness. I've asked God's forgiveness. What more do you want me to do?"

Steve said, "There's got to be some punishment. Somebody's got to pay for what you did!"

Suddenly a light went on in Beth Ann's head. She looked at her husband and said simply, "Somebody did."

Beth Ann remembers, "Months after I admitted I'd been having an affair, this fact sunk into my heart for the very first time: Christ had paid for this! I was forgiven! In forgiveness, there is no punishment, although there have been consequences that Steve and I have had to work through. But God's been with us. We're finally rebuilding our lives."

Lions and Tigers and Bears, Oh My!

Want to tame something ferocious? Something that's been eating you up inside? Something that could impact your relationship with folks you care about?

Then get your whip and chair ready, because here are five steps that can help you show denial who's boss:

Say the words. Twelve-step programs know what they're doing when they ask members to outwit denial by verbalizing the truth: "Hello, my name is Bob, and I'm an alcoholic."

Is there something you've been afraid to admit? "My job is destroying my family; I'm going to have to find a better alternative." "I've been ignoring the signs for months, but I think my teen is on drugs." "My husband isn't merely irresponsible—he's an alcoholic and he needs help." "I think I may be clinically depressed." "I'm going to stop procrastinating and have that lump checked by a professional." Whatever it is, saying the words out loud is a good start.

Research the options. Information has never been so readily available! Make some phone calls, search the Internet, read some literature, talk to someone in the know. Whatever you're facing—stress, health issues, marriage problems, rebellious teens, financial crisis—there are resources available that can help!

Rally support. Rally a network of living, breathing human beings who can encourage you from this point on. Possible resources include personal friends, support groups, professional therapists, siblings, priests or pastors, mentors, or folks from a Bible study or Sunday school class.

Make a plan. You've done your research. You've enlisted a troop of supportive friends and professionals. Now finalize your plan of action. What exactly must you do to experience complete freedom from whatever it is you've been too afraid to admit to anyone, even yourself?

Take action. It takes time to make permanent changes in your life, so get started! In fact, it takes twenty-one days of practicing a new behavior before it starts to turn into a habit, so don't become discouraged if you can't solve your dilemma overnight. When I stopped living in denial about all the weight I had gained, it took me months to significantly change the shape of my body. Counseling takes time. Extracting yourself from toxic relationships takes time. Getting out of financial bondage takes time. Healing takes time, too. But you're on your way; don't stop now!

So much of what you and I struggle with is treatable. Depression is treatable. Stale marriages are treatable. Health problems are treatable. Eating disorders are treatable. Financial woes are treatable.

But if we can't name it, we can't tame it.

There's no shame in living flawed and imperfect lives. Crisis, stress, and dysfunction are not negotiable—they happen to everybody.

The bad news is that denial prolongs the pain.

The good news is that denial is optional.

So nix denial. Choose truth and tell it like it is. It's worth the effort.

Just ask Larry. He couldn't agree more. Especially now that all his friends call him "Mom."

5

....

Body Chemistry 101

Ever wonder what is happening to your brain?
I ask myself that question all the time. Take the other
day, for example, when I looked at my six-year-old and
said, "Kacie, go put the cheese away in the ... the ... you
know. That thing over there. Right there. What's it called
again? Oh yeah. The refrigerator."

Some folks think that memory lapses like this are the result
of middle age. Or artificial sweetener. Or too many hours on
the cell phone. But I have another explanation.

I've read that listening to certain kinds of music can actually alter your brain chemistry. In fact, music not only alters
brain wave patterns, it impacts the autonomic nervous system, hormonal balance, and brain neurotransmitters as well.

This explains a lot, don't you think?

After all, I'm a member of the generation that grew up listening to songs like "Wildfire" and that chart-topping song
by Neil Diamond in which he sings, "'I am,' I said to no one
there, and no one heard, not even the chair." And when I wasn't
humming the tune to "I Shot the Sheriff," I was committing
Barry Manilow songs to memory.

So you can see that I didn't have a chance, really.

And if all that '70s hit music wasn't bad enough, just think about the long-range impact of several hundred episodes of *The Beverly Hillbillies.*

It's enough to make me want to take a sledgehammer to that . . . that thing over there . . . that thingamajig. You know. What's it called again? Oh yeah. I remember. The TV.

Rhythm and the Blues

When I was first diagnosed with clinical depression, my family doctor handed me a prescription. He also gave me some advice: "Exercise for half an hour, three to five times a week. As much good as the medication will do, the exercise will do that much or more."

I thought Prozac and sweat made an odd combination. I know now that it's not so strange after all. Long-term depression can occur as chemistry in the brain gets out of whack. Think of a swimming pool: With the right balance of chemicals, a pool stays clear and clean. But when the chemistry gets out of balance, the pool becomes cloudy and algae-filled, and it can take months to get things balanced again.

The good news is that both medication and exercise impact brain chemistry in a positive way. Medication makes more serotonin available to the brain, while exercise releases feel-good endorphins into your system. That's why both medication and exercise have the power to elevate your mood and make you feel better.

In the years since I was first diagnosed with depression, I've been fascinated with the idea that I can create changes in my brain chemistry and body in a way that elevates my mood and makes me feel better.

As I've said, music can alter brain chemistry. Thus, it provides yet another way to feel good—from the inside out. This is because soothing music really does put us in a different brain wave pattern and lowers our heart rate and blood pressure as well. By the same token, upbeat music also alters our brain waves, heart rate, and energy level. I never attempt to clean my house without some dust-busting, adrenaline-pumping tunes to motivate me into action!

But medication, exercise, and music are only the beginning. Read on for more things you can do that will make you feel better from the inside out.

Increase Your Oxygen Level

An adequate supply of oxygen not only helps our bodies rid themselves of wastes and toxins, but the breathing action of the lungs and diaphragm are the primary pump for the circulation of lymph fluid throughout our systems.

In other words, getting plenty of oxygen keeps us healthier and increases our energy as well.

Unfortunately, you and I are getting less oxygen than our ancestors did. Scientists believe that when the earth was young, the atmosphere contained twice as much oxygen—thirty pounds per square inch versus fifteen today. After the great catastrophic flood, the earth's atmosphere changed dramatically. When that happened, we lost much of the oxygen in our atmosphere—and today's deforestation and pollution have only made things worse.

But when people are put into highly pressurized chambers where the oxygen content is closer to thirty, amazing things happen to their health and well-being. They have tremendous energy. They are less fatigued. They experience increased endurance and, if they happen to get a cut or wound, they benefit from accelerated healing.

Want to feel better and heal better? Increase your intake of oxygen. Not sure how to go about it? Here are three ideas, ranging from conservative to interesting to bizarre.

Just Do It

Aerobic means "with oxygen," and aerobic exercise takes place any time we exercise heartily for twenty minutes or more using the large muscle groups of the body (legs, back, or arms). Biking, swimming, walking, and stairstepping are all good examples of exercises that get our hearts and lungs a-jumpin' and a-pumpin'. The benefits? Increased endorphins, reduced cholesterol and blood pressure, improved muscular endurance, reduced body fat, and increased metabolism. Aerobic exercise also enhances body image, combats depression, and reduces stress.

Take a Deep Breath

If you're not in the mood to sweat, there are any number of exercises you can do to deepen your breathing and get more oxygen into your body. Alternate nostril breathing works just how it sounds: Hold one nostril closed and inhale and exhale slowly and deeply. Then hold the opposite nostril closed and inhale and exhale slowly and deeply. Do this ten or twelve times, several times a day.

A second breathing exercise is to take six normal breaths and then breathe slowly and deeply on the seventh. Do this over an extended period of time—one article I read said that instead of counting breaths, some folks set their digital watches to beep every twenty seconds throughout the day, to remind them to take a deep relaxing breath at that time.

Happy Hour for Heavy Breathers

Okay, I promised we'd go from the conventional to the bizarre, and here it is! In Europe, Asia, and now in major cities in the U.S., oxygen bars are a hot new trend. The web site www.oxygen4u.com describes oxygen bars in this fashion: "You sit next to a large hookah with four sprawling tentacles—"(Wait a minute . . . did I log on to an oxygen bar web site or a web site describing the Star Wars alien-infested Tatooine tavern?)"—like an industrial octopus [with] flasks of water bubbling at the edge of each lim. The oxygen 'aperitif' comes in orange, mint, or lemon. The gaseous cocktail bubbles away as the tubing is wrapped around your ears and put up in your nose."

The cost for this experience is a mere ten dollars for fifteen minutes, unless of course they have to explain to you what a *lim* is, in which case you are charged double. I should probably stop at an ATM before I go.

Chocolate Lovers, Heads Up!

Want to change your body chemistry and feel uplifted as a result? Here's an interesting tidbit from—who else?—Hershey's:

> Chocolate has antioxidants, polyphenols, and flavonoids which are beneficial compounds found in many foods, fruit, cocoa, veggies, and red wine. Scientists say these compounds help reduce the risk of cancer and heart disease, and they have anti-aging benefits. It has [also] been suggested that chocolate consumption may elevate your mood as a result of its content of biologically active compounds. It has also been suggested that people crave chocolate because these compounds affect your mood. One such compound is phenylethylamine, which is a neurotransmitter-like substance. Phenylethylamine also improves moods when administered to certain depressed patients, however, there is no scientific data showing that chocolate consumption has a pharmacological effect.

If you want to feel better, a couple of Kisses may well do the trick. Just keep your binge conservative or else tomorrow's scale may be the bearer of bad news!

A Chuckle a Day Keeps the Doctor Away

We know that a good belly laugh has the power to make us feel better. But do we know *why* we feel so much better after we hoot and guffaw?

Someone has said that laughing is like jogging for our insides. It not only burns calories, it releases endorphins and alters our brain wave patterns. I've often said that laughter makes us healthier in body, mind, and spirit—it relieves stress, enhances communication, and lifts our spirits. It's even been known to prevent certain facial wrinkles. Best of all, it has no calories and can't make us pregnant, so there's no reason why

Laugh Your Way to a Longer, Healthier Life

When you have a good, hearty laugh, your respiratory, glandular, skeletal/muscular, and cardiovascular systems all get exercised. Here's what happens:

Cardiovascular system: When you guffaw, both your heart rate and blood pressure go up. When you stop laughing, they dip below normal. It's very much like aerobic exercise. It's why some researchers call laughing "internal jogging."

Respiratory system: After a hearty laugh, you frequently have to take in a big breath of air. Sometimes you cough. Laughing is good for your respiratory system.

Skeletal/Muscular system: Sometimes you laugh so hard you can hardly get out of your chair. This happens because when you laugh you relax your muscles. In fact, sometimes you relax your muscles so much that you [wet] your pants!

—ALLEN KLEIN, SELF-NAMED "JOLLYTOLOGIST" AND AUTHOR OF
THE HEALING POWER OF HUMOR AND THE COURAGE TO LAUGH

As a medical scientist, it is gratifying and fulfilling to continue to discover objective scientific data to support beliefs that many have held intuitively for centuries: "A merry heart doeth good like a medicine."

—DR. LEE BERK, PROFESSOR
SCHOOLS OF MEDICINE AND PUBLIC HEALTH
LOMA LINDA UNIVERSITY

laughter shouldn't be a first-line defense against the stresses of each day!

Not to mention what it does to our immune systems! Researchers took a group of folks and studied their immune systems before and after watching a humorous video. They discovered that an hour of laughing boosted the immune system by increasing the production of immunoglobulin A, which is found in saliva and blood and is our first line of defense against colds and the flu. Laughing also stimulated bone marrow to produce a significantly greater number of B cells, and increased the activity and the number of natural killer cells, which seek out and destroy tumors and viruses.

Laughter really *is* good medicine.

Love Means Never Having to Say "Gesundheit"

Physiologically, there are so many health benefits to sex that I hardly know where to start. Sex stimulates myriad changes in your brain chemistry and body, which in turn leave you healthier and happier than you were before you got horizontal.

Want the short list? For starters, sex burns calories—approximately 150 calories in thirty minutes! Sex also improves circulation, lowers cholesterol, reduces stress, improves sleep, and even acts as a pain reliever. It staves off symptoms of aging by stimulating production of the hormone DHEA, which enhances the immune system, promotes bone growth, and keeps skin healthy and supple. It boosts testosterone in both men and women, which fortifies bones and muscles, and it also boosts estrogen, which protects against heart disease.

Sex also puts us in touch with the power of, well, touch. Nonsexual touching creates so many healthful effects that one doctor refers to it as "vitamin T." Indeed, touching stimulates a chemical reaction in our bodies that makes us feel good and increases our overall health as well.

Never Say Die

In our ongoing search to experience a positive difference in our lives, here's one more thing we can do that is linked to measurable biochemical changes in our bodies.

And it's simply this: Stay hopeful.

Studies show that when people lose hope, their immune system begins to falter as cells that normally seek and destroy cancerous cells or viruses begin to shut down. Furthermore, in the absence of hope we often give greater rein to anger and fear in our lives, which in turn washes our brains and bodies with a constant flow of powerful "fight or flight" chemicals. "Fight or flight" chemicals are designed to give us the energy to respond quickly to crises in our lives. They are a great expedient measure—an occasional quick-burst, short-term, 911-style solution. But if we stay in a hopeless, angry, or fearful mind-set over the long haul, these powerful chemicals work against us, eroding our immune system and undermining our overall well-being.

Embracing Wellness from Every Angle

A long time ago, a great king acknowledged the following truth, preserved for us in the pages of the Bible. He wrote, "We are fearfully and wonderfully made."

I couldn't have said it better myself. The connections between mind, body, and soul are not merely intriguing, they are the intentional handiwork of a Creator who is as innovative as he is wise.

So the next time you're stressed or hurting, consider doing something that is as good for your body as it is for your emotions. Exercise. Listen to music. Breathe. Eat a little chocolate. Laugh. Make love. And above all, hang on to your hope.

Believe it or not, it's just what the doctor ordered.

6

The Write Stuff

M y friend Beth Forester came over last week, and we spent an hour pondering a rather weighty dilemma.

It all started when we found ourselves complaining about that really weird way our refrigerators have of calling our names. I can't explain it, but it's as if, when I wasn't paying attention, my refrigerator signed up for a correspondence course in mind control. I can be minding my own business, sitting at my desk, watching TV, or folding laundry, when all of a sudden I feel my name being called in a hypnotic fashion from the kitchen.

Remember those old horror movies where Vincent Price cranks up the voltage in his eyes and focuses all of his supernatural mental powers on his victim, who is immediately transformed into a mindless, obedient zombie?

Well, that's exactly what happens to me. I hear my name and find myself drawn magnetically into the kitchen, where I proceed, in an obedient and zombie-esque manner, to eat everything my refrigerator tells me to eat. I still remember the day I called one of my friends and said, "I'm so disgusted with myself! I've just spent the past two days eating everything in sight! Doritos, ice cream, chocolate chips from the bag, graham crackers dipped in chocolate frosting, you name it, I've eaten it! I've been eating blindly and nonstop. Anything in my path has been fair game. Nothing's safe." I paused a moment. "Now that I think about it, the situation may be worse than I thought. I haven't seen our dog since yesterday."

So this was the nature of my conversation with Beth when suddenly she said, "What if we made a list of things we could do *instead* of answering the call of the fridge? What if we got fifty index cards and wrote down fifty alternatives to bingeing? Then, when last night's cobbler is calling our names, we can grab our card file, pick a card at random, and do whatever it says instead of eating!"

It's a great idea. I'll let you know how it works. I haven't tried it yet because I'm still writing out index cards. Actually, it'll probably be a great diet. At this rate, my hand will be so cramped from writing out all these cards that I won't be able to open the refrigerator door.

Or maybe I will. Yesterday the postman delivered a package. It was from the correspondence school, and it was addressed to my refrigerator. Having passed the mind-control course, this ambitious appliance is moving on to bigger things. This semester he's taking a course in electronics.

I think he's building a refrigerator-door remote.

List-Lovers, Unite!

Actually, I think Beth was onto something with her list of pig-out alternatives! This is because there is a certain magic inherent in the simple act of making a list.

Even kids understand the power of list-making. Last December my daughters attached their Christmas wish lists to the refrigerator. Actually, I had to lift the lists to *find* the refrigerator. One night I had to go through so much paperwork to get my hands on a few small leftovers, I thought it was April and I was filing my taxes.

Actually, who am I to complain? I love lists. I love Christmas lists and to-do lists, shopping lists and housework lists, and lists of five-year goals and daily chores. Of all the lists I love to create, my personal favorites are lists of remedies for the problem areas in my life. But I like making lists for others, too.

Beth's Bingeing Alternatives (List One)

Is your refrigerator calling your name? Have you been eyeing your children's stash of Halloween candy? Are you craving an entire box of Cap'n Crunch despite what it would do to the roof of your mouth?

Take heart. Eat an apple and then tackle one of the ideas from the following list. Chances are, by the time you're done, the fructose from the apple will have raised your blood sugar and lowered your cravings. Good luck!

Call a friend
Walk the dog
Call your husband at work and whisper something sexy
Dust the house
Clean out a closet
Go see a movie (sans popcorn!)
Send an e-mail to a friend
Drink water
Drive to the supermarket and buy fresh flowers for your kitchen table
Give yourself a pedicure
Buy a new shade of lipstick
Change the sheets on your bed
Eat lowfat yogurt
Do a load of laundry

My friend Laura and I were driving in her car one day when she admitted that, without a man in her life, she was feeling out of touch with her feminine, sensual side. Incurable listophile that I am, I immediately whipped out a pen and cast about for the nearest piece of paper. (It turned out to be a used envelope, which is not as weird as it might seem: I once wrote a grocery list with a lipstick pencil on a disposable diaper.)

"Okay," I said, "let's make a list of things that make you feel sexy and sensual. Things you can do for yourself, by yourself, with or without a man in your life."

Laura laughed and agreed. By the time we were finished, the list included pedicures, sweaty workouts on a treadmill, healthy eating, a makeover at the cosmetic counter of a local department store, and wearing thong panties.

And Laura isn't the only friend I've tried to "prosel-LIST-ize," so to speak.

Recently, for example, I was speaking at a conference when a woman approached me. We had spent some time together six years before at a conference we attended with our husbands, and it was fun to renew the acquaintance.

While we were chatting, Carol recalled a few things she remembered about me from the first time we met (like the fact that I had blonde hair then, and now I'm a brunette!). But the story I like best was when she said, "I remember I said I'd never been to Dallas, and you immediately began telling me about all the fun things there are to do in the city. Then you had me make a list of the restaurants and attractions you were telling me about so I'd remember them if I ever found myself in Dallas."

I laughed. "I actually made you make a list?"

"Yep."

"And I'd known you, what, all of about three hours?"

"Yep."

You know, there are support groups for everything nowadays. I should see if there's any help for people like me.

Then again, maybe having a list fetish is not such a bad thing after all.

List-making has a certain power all its own. When we make a list, we're taking the intangible and putting it in the palm of

Beth's Bingeing Alternatives (List Two)

Go to the gym

Call someone who needs encouragement

Give someone a compliment

Make love to your husband

Eat five bites of something rich and fattening and delicious

Put on your favorite CD and dance

Sit on the porch and drink coffee from your most elegant china

Take a bath

Eat an apple and a stick of lowfat Mozzarella cheese

Paint your nails

Chew gum

Call your best laughing-buddy and have a silly conversation until you're enjoying a good belly laugh

Grab old magazines, scissors, and glue, and make a collage—you pick the theme. (Need some ideas? How about dream vacations, cute kids, clothing/makeup styles you'd love to try, decorating ideas, images that remind you of your childhood, things that are green, images that make you happy, pictures of what heaven might be like ... you get the idea!)

Eat a bag of fat-free microwave popcorn

Log on to the Internet and research your dream vacation

Bleach the hair on your arms and upper lip

Do one thing you've been putting off for months

Play the piano

our hand. If it's writeable, it's graspable. And if it's graspable, it's probably pretty close to doable.

The truth is, list-making is underrated, getting far less applause and kudos than it deserves. It is, after all, a little bit of magic in a world where magic is on the wane.

And all for the price of a Bic pen.

Feeling Grumpy? Make a List!

Maybe you're feeling burned out from the hectic pace of everyday living. Maybe you're facing a crisis of some sort and it's got you feeling grumpy and overwhelmed. Or perhaps you're in deep emotional pain from past wounds that just won't heal.

Whether the crisis you're experiencing is in your surroundings, your schedule, or your soul, I encourage you to begin to tame the chaos by grabbing a piece of paper and penning a list. Here are three kinds of lists that I write when I'm trying to get the upper hand with stress or pain in my life:

Sometimes I write a list to *organize* my thoughts, activities, or priorities. My daily to-do list falls into this category, brimming with directives like "Go to the bank" or "Write for three hours before lunch" or "Clean out all the Happy Meal wrappers from the van."

Other times I create lists of ideas to *solve* a problem in my life. For example, to solve my problem of arriving late all the time, I might create a list of possible solutions such as "Set all your clocks ahead two hours," "Get completely dressed the night before," "Hire a personal assistant armed with an electric cattle prod," or "Go live in a primitive culture where timeliness is a foreign concept."

Finally, sometimes I create lists of ways to *cope*. Actually, my book *Just Hand Over the Chocolate and No One Will Get Hurt* evolved from this kind of list. Nancy Rottmeyer and I were sitting in a booth at The Brass Bean coffee shop and discussing our personal battles with stress and depression when suddenly I said, "So how can we cope? What are ways we can feel better?" I wrote our ideas on a napkin. We talked about gardening and whining. We talked about forgiving grudges, pursuing our dreams, and taking better care of our bodies. These ideas and others became the foundation for *Just Hand Over the Chocolate*. And now the book you're reading this very minute carries on that tradition with *new* ways to feel better!

I think every woman needs to have in her possession precisely that kind of a list. Every woman needs her own list of things she can do that will make a positive difference in her life emotionally, physically, or spiritually.

In fact, let me tell you about a time not long ago when I sat down and wrote out that kind of a list for myself, and how it got me through one of the darkest, scariest seasons of my life.

Need a Life Preserver? Make a List!

Two years ago I embarked on one of the most terrible and amazing seasons of my life. Earlier in this book I admitted that long-term denial had landed me in a heap of emotional pain and crisis. I know I told you that my emotional pain felt like an ocean inside of me, but I've been thinking about that analogy. Maybe ocean is not the right word. Maybe emotional pain is more like a lake. Maybe Lake Michigan, which is so huge that it has weather patterns all its own and waves and tidal activity just like any other sea.

I'm suggesting that emotional pain is more like a lake, because you can dam up a lake. I'm beginning to think there needs to be a dam somewhere in this word picture, because that's exactly what it felt like. Two years ago, somewhere inside of me, a dam burst, and tidal waves of anger and pain that had been accumulating for much of my seventeen-year marriage flooded my world.

Now, it takes a while for flood waters to subside. (Just ask Noah!) In the meantime, there's the potential for lots of destruction to take place. On many days the swirling waters and debris-ridden currents threatened to suck me under. On other days my anger and pain were so consuming that I would literally roam the house, room to room, looking for something, anything, that would provide a temporary distraction from my grief. I was looking for a raft—any raft—that would keep me afloat for just another hour or two.

One day Larry walked into my office where I was sitting at my computer. I closed out a screen as he approached, but it was too late.

"What was that?" he asked. "What were you doing?"

I winced. "I was in a chat room. I was flirting with a total stranger online."

Larry stared at me like I had just morphed into Mikhail Gorbachev or something. "You were WHAT? Why in the world would you do that?"

I looked him in the eye. "Because the attention felt really good. Because I'm really hurting right now, and it felt really, really good."

What I soon discovered is that without even trying, I had come up with a list of ways to feel better. Actually, two lists. These lists were invisible because I had yet to write them down, but they were very real nevertheless.

Each list contained things I turned to when my pain and anger over my wounded marriage became too great to bear. These were the things I sought in order to keep my head above water. These were my life rafts. One of my lists contained things that were positive and healthy and helpful. The other contained things that were not.

I realized this one afternoon when Larry said wistfully, "I know you've said for years that our marriage is in trouble, and that I've ignored your cries for help. But I'm not ignoring you now. Is it too late? You've withdrawn so far from me. I feel like you're not trying at all. Why can't you work harder on our marriage?"

I began to cry. "Work harder? You have no idea how hard I'm working just to cope. It's like I have one set of coping strategies that are destructive, strategies like eating everything in sight, flirting with men online, or sitting on the couch for hours and just giving in to depression. Then I have these other strategies that *aren't* destructive. Things like running out the door to the gym and working the tread off some unsuspecting treadmill, writing in my journal, playing the piano, scheduling a counseling appointment, or calling a girlfriend in a panic at eleven at night and saying, 'I feel like I'm going crazy! Can you meet me for coffee?' And every day it's

Fourteen (More!) Ways to Feel Better

This book lists more than a dozen ways to experience a positive difference in your life. Below you'll find fourteen additional ideas for your emotional, physical, and spiritual wellness, taken from the pages of the book *Just Hand Over the Chocolate and No One Will Get Hurt:*

Plant something
Take a mini-vacation
Spend time with girlfriends
Learn how to get the most out of a fine whine
Sing TV theme songs with a friend
Rekindle your dreams
Simplify your life
Protect your privacy
Forgive someone who hurt you
See a professional counselor
Believe in magic
Guard your thoughts
Take care of your body
Tend to your soul

all I can do to muster my strength to pick from the second set and not the first. Some days I succeed. And other days I don't."

Tears pooled in Larry's eyes, and he put his arms around me. "You really are trying, aren't you?" he said. "I never understood how wounded you've been by our marriage. I wish I had listened to you sooner. I'm so sorry."

As he held me, I wondered if there would come a day when I would have the energy to care about our marriage again. All I knew was that, right then, saving our marriage was the farthest thing from my mind. Strong currents of unforgiven hurts were threatening to pull me under for the third time, and I was no longer fighting for our relationship. I was fighting for my life.

Eventually I sat down and put into words all the ways I was coping with my pain. I wrote everything down—the healthy choices and the destructive choices.

It was a good start. Now I had a plan. Something to follow. Every day I worked hard to make the healthiest choices I could. A lot of days I failed, but eventually I began to see some progress. I began to have hope. I was still floundering, but I was also getting a few strokes in now and again. Maybe one day I would make shore after all.

Pain Management 101

I love the "Dummies" series of books, don't you? I think it started with *Windows for Dummies,* and to date I've seen books on everything from auto repair to taxes to romance.

The titles promise it all: instruction that is so basic, so foundational, so elementary, that folks with the same IQ as zucchini should be able to understand the principles and apply them to their lives.

Wouldn't it be great if there was a book entitled *Pain Management for Dummies?* Chapter One could be titled "Don't Treat a Headache with a Hammer," and we could build from there.

Because that's sometimes what we do, isn't it? We treat headaches with hammers. Sometimes when we're in pain, our remedies can cause as much pain—or even more!—as the wounds they were designed to treat.

That's what happened to me. In my pain, I was chasing solutions—food, chat rooms, even an occasional sleeping pill to escape—that were supposed to *ease* my pain but were *compounding* it instead!

I can't encourage you enough to make a plan. Even if you're not in an emotional crisis at this very moment, what will you do when you are? Where will you turn? How will you spell R-E-L-I-E-F? Be prepared with a list of constructive ways to handle stress and pain in your life.

I've already given you most of my "healthy" list. It included going to the gym, writing in my journal, and making and keeping appointments with a counselor. I spent time with my girlfriends and my family. Some days when no one was home, I expressed my sorrow and anger through music, playing the piano so forcefully that my fingertips would feel sore for days.

One night I put on one of my favorite CDs—Susan Ashton's *A Distant Call*—turned out all the lights, and danced by myself in the living room. Other nights I cried. Sometimes I prayed. I even started attending church on Sunday nights. I'd like to say it was because I got so much out of the sermons, but the truth is that I was in too much pain to be able to concentrate on anything our pastor had to say. Instead, I was drawn to the place where I knew God had been waiting for me. I didn't always say much to him when I got there, but somehow it was healing just even being in the same room with him.

When we're in crisis, can we choose healthy ways to ease the pain as we look for a path back to wholeness? The answer is yes.

Start writing. Choose wisely. Pursue wholeness.

If I can do it, you can, too.

Beth's Bingeing Alternatives (List Three)

Put peanut butter on your pet's tongue

Browse a book of Dilbert cartoons

Write in your journal

Eat a banana and drink a glass of skim milk

Research your family tree

Shave your legs

Call a parent or grandparent and ask them to tell you a story about their childhood. Tape the conversation for yourself, your siblings, or your kids

Apply sunless tanning lotion to your body

Pray for your friends and family

Blindfold your eyes, then draw a simple shape like a flower, box, or house

Drive to a farmer's market in your town and buy bags of fresh fruits and veggies

Log on to Victoriasecret.com and order something sexy

Do something weird to your hair

Make five chocolate kisses last for half an hour

Get in your car and go for a drive. Don't plan a route—just turn down any street that looks interesting (but don't end up at Dairy Queen)

Make plans to go to a nice restaurant for a healthy dinner

Eat something low in fat and high in protein

Buy a floor plan book and pick out your dream house

7

Sister, Can You Spare a Whine?

'll never forget the week my sister Renee Berge flew to Dallas for a visit. The days were filled with a flurry of warm-fuzzy, memory-making Kodak moments. Renee and I not only caught up on the details of each other's lives, we enjoyed watching our young kids—her sons Conner, Hunter, and Isaac, and my daughters Kaitlyn and Kacie—rediscover the joys of cousinhood after nearly a year apart.

I collected lots of warm family memories from that week.

For instance, there was the bonding that took place between Renee and me as we honed our teamwork, working side by side to scrub Hunter's crayoned artwork from the stairwell walls before Larry got home from work. To this day he doesn't realize that there's no paint on half the stairwell wall. What he *thinks* is paint is actually the drywall. We were lucky it was only a shade away from the color the paint used to be before it all got scrubbed off with cleanser.

Another warm family memory is the time Renee and I were in the kitchen making some sort of dessert that called for crushed vanilla wafers. I was beginning to dig around for my rolling pin when Renee grabbed the box of cookies and my car keys and headed out the front door. "Don't worry—"she hollered behind her, "I'll take care of it."

The kids, sensing adventure, followed her onto the porch.

She returned several minutes later and handed me the cookies. They were beautifully crushed, although the box didn't look so hot.

"What'd you do?" I asked.

"I wedged the box behind the right front tire of your van and then popped the engine into reverse."

"YOU RAN OVER THE COOKIES?"

She glanced at the recipe before heading toward the refrigerator for the next ingredient on the list. I got there first. "You did great with the cookies," I said with admiration, "but maybe you should let me handle the eggs."

Boomerang Problems

I admire my sister's creative talent for solving problems. She's lucky she has that gift, because life is filled with problems, isn't it? They range from "Great, I can't find the rolling pin" to "The doctor says it's malignant" to "He's filing for divorce." From the trivial to the traumatic, problems seem to be the stuff of life.

Which is probably why I have this thing for solutions. I crave them, write about them, search for them, cherish them, glean them from others, and admire the chutzpah of anyone who comes up with a really innovative one (such as Renee's interpretation of a six-cylinder minivan as a kitchen gadget).

But if you're like me, you realize that finding a really good solution is a little like shopping for the right bathing suit: You've got to try out a lot of "uh-uh, no-ways" before you find your miracle.

Sometimes I get tired. I've got a few problems that I just can't seem to permanently solve, no matter how hard I try. Problems that are as tenacious as a pit bull, as dependable as a boomerang. Problems that even Renee—armed with every kitchen gadget imaginable, leaded and unleaded alike—would be hard pressed to solve for me.

My weight falls into this category. I'm making some progress but not as quickly as I'd like. Last year, for example, I lost sixty pounds. The good news is that I've kept that weight off for more than a year. The bad news is that I get discouraged because I still need to lose about forty more and I can't seem to climb down off this plateau. Still, I remind myself that just staying at this weight for a year has been a huge accomplishment. I haven't maintained any weight for years—I've either been gaining or losing. So I'm thankful that I'm finally learning some new patterns.

But I'd still like to beat this battle once and for all, and so far that hasn't happened.

So I get discouraged.

There are also some quicksand pits in my marriage that I've been trying to shore up and fill in for years. Always the same ones. You know, Larry and I seem to be fairly intelligent people, so why can't we get these problems solved once and for all? Why can't we get with the program? I'm still looking for the answer to that one.

Depression is another familiar nemesis. Nine years ago I hit rock bottom. Prozac, counseling, and the prayers of folks who loved me helped me crawl out of that pit. It took a while, but eventually life was fun again. Then three years ago I felt myself slipping back into the pit. I went to my husband and said, "Larry, I feel like the depression is right behind me and it's gaining ground. I'm overwhelmed and I feel like I'm slipping. Please help me!" We brainstormed together and came up with a list of ways to reduce stress in our lives. It helped. It kept the monster at bay.

I thought.

A year later I thought I was doing okay. I wasn't a depressed slob like I'd been back in '91. I was working out at the gym, eating fairly healthy, and wearing makeup and cute clothes. So when my friend Beth told me I was still struggling with depression, I told her she was crazy. But the more I thought about her words, the more I realized she was right. I was sleeping too much. I couldn't concentrate on even simple tasks. I wasn't able to write or meet deadlines. I felt sad or overwhelmed much of the time. Sure, I had one area of my life where I seemed to be functioning with some success, but the rest of my life was a mess.

I took action. I got back into counseling, began taking some herbs and vitamins, and made other changes to get back on track.

I guess I'd never expected that my depression would come back. And yet I shouldn't have been surprised. Doctors say that a majority of folks who are diagnosed with clinical depression will experience a recurrence at some point in their lives. The good news is that each time it happens I'm getting smarter about recognizing the symptoms, even if they look a little different than they did before. And each time my struggle is less severe than before.

But it remains a familiar battle. Bummer, huh?

My point is not to whine (although I think I did a pretty good job, don't you?). All I'm saying is that you and I have some problems in our lives that don't lend themselves to quick fixes, and sometimes our ongoing search for healthy, permanent solutions can leave us feeling fatigued.

But this book is about feeling better, right? This book is about things we can do that will make a positive difference in our lives. This book is about solutions, so there must be *something* we can do, even when we're being dogged by stubborn dilemmas in our lives.

And there is.

When you're feeling worn out from wrestling with seemingly insurmountable problems in your life, pick up the phone, call a friend, and borrow a whine.

Making a Positive Difference with Pepperoni

Borrowing a whine has worked in my life. Let me give you an example. About a year ago I was really struggling. Every day was the same. Every day I fought the same battles. One morning I woke up and thought, "Enough is enough. I need a mental change of scenery!"

It dawned on me that my friend Nancy Rottmeyer was returning home with her family after being out of town for a week. No doubt they'd appreciate a few grocery-store staples—milk, bread, some fruit, maybe even a plate of cookies—waiting for them in their kitchen.

I remembered that my friend Darla Talley had been feeding the Rottmeyers' dog, so she had a key to the house. She could let me in!

I grabbed my phone and punched in Darla's number.

When she said "Hello" I was tempted to ask "Who died?" She sounded about as tired and worn out as the upholstery on my favorite thinking chair (circa 1966).

Instead I asked, "What's wrong?"

She said, "Mike's out of town, and I'm supposed to finish packing up the house so we can move into our new place across town by Monday. I'm out of packing paper, I've called three places in town and they're sold out, I don't have time to go pick any up anyway, there are boxes everywhere, and I'm feeling really overwhelmed."

I stifled a giggle. "I'll be there in an hour."

I called around and found packing paper. I ordered pizza. I showed up at Darla's house with both. We packed. We laughed. We bolstered our strength with pepperoni pizza and Pepsi.

I never did make it to Nancy's house that day (sorry, Nancy!). But when I fell into my bed that night, I felt great. Tired, sore, a little dusty, but great.

I can't solve the world's problems. A lot of the time I can't even solve my own dilemmas. But every now and then I come across a problem I *can* solve. Darla's problem was like that. It was easy. I had the time. I had the resources. I could do it!

So I did. And you know what? It felt GREAT!

Are you in a rut? Stuck with personal problems you have yet to solve? Look around. Somewhere, in the life of someone near you, there's a problem you *can* solve. Borrow it for a couple of hours. Solve it, or at least give its owner a little relief. Your friend will feel better and you will, too.

And who knows? Maybe someday someone will do the same for you. Maybe you'll find yourself with a pressing need, and when you least expect a miracle, a good Samaritan will come along with just the right touch.

Even if they have to use a four-thousand-pound minivan to do it.

Renee's Recipe for Texas Dirt Cups

1. Run over a box of chocolate vanilla wafers with a large motorized vehicle, several times if necessary.

2. Spoon a layer of crushed cookies into bottom of small clear plastic cup.

3. Spoon prepared chocolate pudding into the cup on top of the crumbs.

4. Top with another layer of cookie crumbs.

5. Stick a plastic flower and a candy worm into the "dirt."

8

....

Tell a Secret

Ever notice how some things take on a life of their own?

The dust under my bed tends to do this. Some people have dust bunnies. I, on the other hand, have a dust community. And it's thriving. At night I hear them building roads under there. Last month they voted on a mayor. I understand they even have a senior citizens' home. Their motto is, "Old Dirt Needs Love, Too."

Other things that can take on lives of their own include overdue bills and lunch boxes left in lockers over summer vacation.

Some household projects fit into this category as well. I'll never forget the morning I woke up, swung my legs out of bed, and planted my feet in two inches of water. A pipe connected to the dishwasher had apparently busted during the night and flooded the house. We fixed the pipe and ripped up all the water-logged carpet. While the carpet was out, we decided it was the perfect time to remove a wall between the den and living room that we'd always hated. This opened up the house beautifully but meant there was no longer a good place to put our couch. Obviously, we had no choice but to replace my grandmother's hand-me-down couch with a couple of brand-new love seats. And naturally, with no place to put Mamaw's couch, we were forced to call a contractor and build a room addition.

I'm kidding. But only about the room addition. Everything else is true. That one broken pipe really did evolve into new carpet, a new doorway, and new furniture. (The good news is that Larry never suspected a thing. I'm lucky he never thought to dust the pipe wrench for my fingerprints!)

There's something else that can take on a life of its own. I'm talking about a secret.

Ever notice how a really juicy secret begs to be told? It's as if it takes on a life of its own, demanding to be passed along. Some people, however, can take secrets to their grave. I could do that, too, but you'd have to tell me and then kill me immediately.

No, no, I'm kidding. (I can imagine all my friends who have told me their deepest secrets reading this and cringing.) I never tell other people's secrets. But my own are certainly hard to keep.

The secrets of other members in my family are also fair game.

Kaitlyn has learned this. She knows that her secrets are liable to show up in one of my books, articles, or speeches. Some days, after she has just said or done something cute or embarrassing, she looks at me and says, "All right, I guess you can use this one." Other days she shoots me a stern glare and warns, "Don't even *think* about it."

Some secrets are more fun to share than others. Beauty secrets fit into this category. Recently, for example, I swapped secrets with a friend. I showed Diane how to bleach the hair on her arms, and she showed me how to wax my upper lip.

One of the strangest beauty secrets I've ever heard was when Terri Ann Kelly admitted to me that she has, on occasion, replaced missing shoulder pads with feminine hygiene products.

I had a chance to try this out a couple months ago when I pulled a jacket from my closet and realized one shoulder pad was missing. I wasted fifteen minutes excavating the floor of my closet before remembering her suggestion, going into the bathroom, opening the cabinet and grabbing a couple of Kotex. They not only worked great but provided a wonderful ice breaker at the party I attended. This is because partygoers have a tendency to loosen up a bit after a fellow guest drapes her jacket over a seat, removes it several minutes later, and leaves a sanitary napkin taped to the back of her chair in the process.

But I guess Terri Ann's not the only woman with an unorthodox beauty secret. If truth be told, I have my own array of strange beauty practices. Like, for example, plucking unwanted facial hairs. I used to spend lots of time peering into my dimly lit bathroom mirror and wielding tweezers. Then one day I realized the sunlight in my car made the little suckers easier to see, while stoplights provided minutes that would be otherwise wasted. So now I keep tweezers in my car and take care of business on the road. Of course, the downside is that our gas expenses have doubled. This is because friends and family prefer to drive second cars everywhere we go.

Which gives me a whole new appreciation for my community of dust bunnies. They may make me sneeze, but they're pretty unconditional in their devotion. They love me even if I pluck chin hairs in public, scatter sanitary napkins at parties, or tell all their secrets in my books. The only thing that might end our friendship would be if I turned a new leaf and began taking housecleaning seriously.

I think we're in for a long and happy friendship.

Thanks for Sharing

Now when it comes to telling secrets, we would be wise to use a little discretion. For example, don't tell your deepest secrets to a coworker whose nickname around the office happens to be Speed-Dial Donna.

It's also wise to avoid airing dirty laundry to casual acquaintances who, quite frankly, don't need or want to know. My sister Michelle, for example, was giving a bridal shower for her friend Jenny. One evening a woman on the guest list called Michelle to RSVP. The woman said, "I'm planning to come to the party, although it's hardly a secret that Jenny *did* have sex with my husband, Mark." My sister was dumbfounded until she remembered that years ago, before his marriage, Mark had dated Jenny. Actually, after Michelle remembered this bit of trivia, she was *still* speechless at the too-candid confession from the total stranger on the other end of the phone line.

Maybe we should call this the "Godiva Syndrome." Not, of course, Godiva as in chocolate—heaven knows that's a syndrome I'd be more than willing to endure—but Godiva as in the woman who rode naked through the town square.

It's possible to bare too much, and to the wrong folks.

We should divulge our secrets on a need-to-know basis. And sometimes there are things in our lives other folks just don't need to know.

Having said all that, there are times when an untold secret refuses to lie quietly and well-behaved in our souls. There are times when, as in the case of my broken pipe, an untold secret begins as a small thing, but one thing leads to another until it manages to impact every part of our lives.

Remember when you were a kid and you were afraid to swallow any watermelon seeds, for fear they would sprout in your stomach and pretty soon you'd have vines coming out of your ears? Oh. You never thought that? Must have been just me. But in any case, most of us realize by now that watermelon seeds don't work that way.

Secrets, on the other hand, do.

Literary greats have realized this truth. Edgar Allan Poe has always managed to hold me spellbound with his story *The Tell-Tale Heart.* Perhaps you too remember the story of the man who murdered someone and hid the body under the floorboards of his home. He had committed the perfect crime: no witnesses, no evidence, no trail of clues. He was home free. What he hadn't counted on, however, was the fact that secrets can be unruly little critters. They have minds of their own and tend to thrive in dark places. Before the end of the story, the murderer ends up throwing himself at a policeman and screaming his confession. Was he under interrogation? Had the long arm of the law finally caught up with him? Not at all. He wasn't even a suspect! He simply could no longer stand the incessant, accusing voice of the secret thriving in the darkness of his soul.

Confession Is Good for the Soul

Sometimes, when we find ourselves grumpy, stressed, or hurting, it's possible that a harbored secret is to blame. So let me ask you a question: Is there a hidden wound or unspoken failure in your life that is keeping you from experiencing hope, healing, passion, and joy in your life? I have seen numerous examples of how telling a secret can lift a tremendous burden.

A woman I met at a conference confided that she'd had an affair. She said that even when the affair had been over for a year, she remained in bondage to guilt and pain until the day she bared her soul to a friend. She admitted, "The day after I told my friend about my affair, I was filled with panic and dread. I thought, *What have I done! What if she tells other people?* But she never told, and her love for me never wavered either. Looking back, I can see that my confession was the beginning of healing for me. My secret had been eating me alive, but after I told someone, its power began to wane."

I was in a prayer meeting when a woman stood and addressed the friends and acquaintances in the room. Her voice quivered as she said, "I've never told a soul, but I know I can't bear it alone any longer. I had an abortion five years ago, and I've never been able to get over the tremendous sense of loss and pain." She had been standing by herself, but suddenly women all over the room rose and made their way to her side. As loving arms embraced her, she began to cry. She wasn't alone anymore.

One day a close friend and I were talking about how hard it is to lose weight. I was saying that we are lovable regardless of our waist size when this woman said, "No. I'm not lovable." I told her I loved her, but she said, "That's because there's something you don't know about me. I have one secret. No one knows what it is, not a single soul. It's the thing that makes me unlovable."

We were both silent a moment, and then she said quietly, "Sometimes I think that the day I get the courage to tell my secret will be the day I finally stop abusing myself with food."

Taking a Calculated Risk

I'll be the first to admit that there are plenty of women who have shared something personal from their lives and then lived to rue the day they did! Their experience didn't lead to healing at all; instead, they were judged or scolded or blackmailed or made the topic of gossip.

I can't promise that will never happen to you. But quite honestly, it's a risk we HAVE to take. Because the alternative is to live in bondage to our secrets, which make pretty cruel taskmasters. And that's a life I don't want to live, thankyouverymuch, and my guess is that you don't either.

The good news is that there are ways you and I can protect ourselves. There are certain signs we should look for that can help us decide when to spill our guts and when to bite our tongues.

So how can we find a "safe" person with whom we can share our secrets? Here are some places to start:

A professional therapist or counselor is a safe bet. These folks don't gossip, they're good listeners, and I can promise you they won't be shocked by anything you have to say (they've heard much worse!). Best yet, they've got a lot of years of education behind them, which means they probably have some fairly sound advice they can pass along your way.

🐚 A trusted spiritual advisor can also be a good choice. A pastor, priest, Sunday school leader, or prayer warrior in your congregation can be a good listener and a solid source of comfort and wisdom.

🐚 How about a complete stranger? Okay, I know this one's weird, but bear with me here a minute. A man told me he once sat next to a woman on a plane, and when their conversation touched on spiritual things, she asked, "Are you a Christian?" He confessed, "My wife and family think I am. But the truth is I'm motivated only by money, I flirt with women when I travel, and I'm not even sure there is a God." He said he figured his secret was safe with this stranger because he would never see her again. And he didn't. But she said she would pray for him in the coming months, and she must have done it, too, because following his confession he began seeking changes in his life. Today he is living the life other folks thought he was living all along; he is a man of integrity, enjoying genuine relationships with the people he loves.

🐚 A close friend or family member is an obvious possibility when you need to get a secret off your chest. When considering baring your heart to someone you know, ask yourself these questions:

"Does she keep other people's confidences or does she love to talk about other people's secrets?" If she tells others' secrets, she'll probably tell yours, too.

"Does she tell me about her own failures, fears, or struggles?" If not, she may feel uncomfortable with that kind of honesty coming from you.

"Does she share my values? Can I trust her advice?" If you don't typically agree with her values or the decisions she makes

for her own life, you might think twice before blindly adopting her advice for your situation.

Unpack Those Deadly Secrets

About twelve years ago I cowrote a book with my good friend Keith Wall. Entitled *Deadly Secrets*, the book told the true story about a young man who lived a secret homosexual lifestyle and eventually contracted AIDS.

Now fast-forward about four years. Larry had just accepted a position at Dallas Baptist University. We had spent weeks packing everything in sight and we were excited about making the move from California to Texas.

I remember the day we loaded up the U-Haul with all our belongings. What an exhausting job that was!

Luckily for us, we had friends and family who showed up to give us a hand. My sister Michelle came and brought with her a young man she had just started dating.

We'd been slinging boxes all morning when we stopped to order pizza for lunch. We were sitting on the floor in the den, balancing paper plates and cups, when Michelle mentioned to her friend, Paul, that I was a writer.

He said, "Really? Cool. What have you written?"

"Probably nothing you've seen. Several books. One called *Working Women, Workable Lives*. I helped on another called *The Woodland Hills Tragedy*. Cowrote another called *Deadly Secrets*."

Suddenly Paul began to laugh. He looked relieved. Michelle stared at her friend. "What's so funny?" she finally asked.

He had to catch his breath before he could speak. "When I was loading boxes into the truck, I got sorta concerned when I saw several boxes labeled 'deadly secrets.' I kept wondering what I'd find next. Maybe 'skeletons from the closet'?"

Michelle and Paul didn't date long after that. Maybe he didn't believe my explanation about the box of deadly secrets and wasn't so sure he wanted to continue dating the normal girl with the weird family (I guess he wouldn't have been comfortable with Marilyn Munster either).

In any case, my box of *Deadly Secrets* got to Texas.

And to be honest, those are the only deadly secrets I keep around. The other kind are too treacherous. I always find somebody I can talk to—my sisters, my mom and dad, my best girlfriends, my husband, guy friends who are like brothers to me, professional counselors—folks who can listen, love me, encourage me, hold me accountable, and sometimes just hold me.

So if you want to know one of my secrets to feeling better when life gets me down, that's it. I just told you.

Don't harbor deadly secrets. Tell someone you can trust.

I suggest you leave Speed-Dial Donna off the list.

9

···

Fall in Love with Your Kids

Every now and then I get a little grumpy. What with daily stresses, the pressures of parenting, work deadlines, housework, relationship glitches, and my occasional dance with depression, sometimes I'm hard to live with.

And that's *before* PMS.

I'm sure you're shocked. No doubt you've been thinking I'm pretty near perfect. Sort of a bionic blend of the best of Martha Stewart and Roma Downey. But denial never did anyone any good (except maybe Egyptian farmers), so I guess we should face the facts.

I remember one night, when Kaitlyn was about nine, engaging in the typical bedtime strategies and war games that make parenting so . . . well, so very interesting.

I had just tucked Kaitlyn under the covers and returned to the living room where Larry and I were in the middle of a game of Rummikub with friends Jerry and Cherie Spurlock. That's when it began:

"Mom . . . I'm thirsty, I need a drink."

"Mom . . . I'm cold, I need another blanket."

"Mom . . . I forgot to brush my teeth. Can I go brush my teeth?"

"Mom . . . I forgot to tell you something important from school today."

"Mom . . . I have to go to the bathroom."

My response? I granted water, retrieved blankets, encouraged dental hygiene, listened politely to news about the upcoming school fundraiser, grudgingly allowed one last potty break, and issued a few stern warnings in the process.

I had just plopped back down on the couch when Kaitlyn—YET AGAIN—hollered down the stairs, "Mom . . ."

Exasperated, I snapped, "Kaitlyn, *shut up!*"

Without missing a beat, Kaitlyn said (was it my imagination or was there a note of smugness in her voice?), "Okay, but I was *just* going to ask you to come pray with me."

I wonder if they give frequent flier miles for guilt trips.

Truth is, I hate it when I get grumpy. I hate it even more when I get grumpy at my kids (even though they're not incapable of pushing a few buttons now and then!).

Now this isn't a book on parenting; it's a book about feeling better. But I think there's a way to kill two birds with one stone, so to speak. I believe there are times when we can elevate our mood *and* improve our parenting at the same time. The reason this is possible is because of the incredible, wonderful, magical power of love.

Mad about You?

Love feels great, doesn't it?

All facets of love are wonderful, but my personal favorite is falling in love. There's just something rejuvenating and exhilarating about it. I'd even go so far as to say that, for her emotional and spiritual well-being, a woman should fall in love, oh, say, two or three times a year.

Now, before you run out the door in search of a man (and blaming me in the process!), let me clarify something: I believe that we can experience the benefits of being in love with or without a man in our lives. This is because—whether we're in love with a lover, a hobby, a pet, or a cause—we just feel more *alive* when we feel passionate about someone or something.

One year I fell in love with my garden. Now, as a rule, I'm not good with plants; some of my most successful experiences with green, growing things have been Chia Pets and bread mold. But suddenly I felt passionate about mulch. I took gardening books to bed with me and scoured nurseries for just the right plants, meaning something hardy with masochistic tendencies.

Another year I fell in love with garage sales. My friend Belinda and I had a system: We grabbed the Friday morning paper, then made a beeline for my kitchen table, where we cut out every garage sale ad and glued it onto an index card. Then we scoured a map for directions, which we wrote on the back of each card before hitting the streets. We were more than serious. More than passionate. Actually, the word *militant* comes to mind.

And when I take on a new book project, there's always a time when I fall in love with my work. I think constantly about the ideas I want to communicate. I fantasize about new chapters when I'm taking a shower, driving carpool, and folding laundry. I love to talk about the book's concepts with anyone who will listen—family, friends, even telemarketers hoping to make a sale if they spend fifteen minutes listening to the crazy woman in Duncanville, Texas. I feel energized by what I'm doing, and I'm passionate about what is being created on the written page.

Gardens, garage sales, and careers are just three examples. Actually, you can write your own list. What do *you* love? What people or activities evoke not just your interest but your passion?

When life has made you grumpy, how can you begin to experience greater healing, hope, passion, and joy in your life? I say, fall in love.

And if you happen to be a parent, a great place to start may be with your very own kids.

Who Loves Ya, Baby?

It's easy to fall in love with our kids when they're babies, isn't it? After all, there's something incredibly enchanting about all those tiny translucent fingers and pink rosebud lips.

Of course, babies never sleep when they're supposed to, and they produce a variety of bodily substances impervious to every known stain remover on the market today. And I haven't even mentioned diapers yet. I have two children, and if I had a dollar for every diaper I've changed, my net worth would be something even Thurston Howell III could get excited about.

But none of those things matter when you're in love. When our babies gaze at us with adoring eyes, coo our names, and pat our cheeks with chubby fingers, something inside of us just melts.

We're smitten.

But as our kids grow, they learn all sorts of new things, like how to talk back, roll their eyes when we ask them to do something, and push all our hot buttons. Within a few years, those adorable baby nurseries we decorated are sporting a grunge motif, and the precious toddlers who won our hearts have been replaced by adolescent-shaped aliens with bad attitudes.

What happens then to the relationship with our kids? Do we still *love* our children? Absolutely. After all, we wash their socks, screen their friends, supervise their chores. We commit ourselves to their growth and well-being. We would give our lives for them. But are we *in love* with them? Do we feel emotionally connected with our kids? Relish their witty remarks? Cherish our time together? Hang on their words as they tell us stories from their day? When we're together, do we feel joy?

If you're like me, sometimes you do, and sometimes you don't. Parenting is hard work. Now and then I'd love a vacation from it all. Yet despite my feelings, my commitment to my children wins out.

I commend the mom who, after a long day, overrides her overwhelming desire to flee to Mexico and instead takes her children to Chuck E. Cheese's for some madhouse memory-making. I admire the mother whose every nerve is screaming for Calgon as she tells her preschooler through clenched jaws, "Of course I'll read *I'm a Bunny* one more time, Tommy."

The Romance of Parenting

Being motivated by commitment is a legitimate expression of love. But to grow the best memories, our kids have to know that sometimes we seek out their company, not because we know we should but because we just can't resist. They need to know we're not merely *committed to them* but *crazy about them*. So how can we enrich our relationships with our kids and rediscover the romance of parenting?

I've got an idea. What if we looked at some of the dynamics that make it so easy to fall in love with our kids when they're babies and apply these same principles to our parenting at every stage? I think we'll be thrilled with the results, and so will our children.

So here they are: five suggestions that can help us fall in love with our kids at every age and stage.

Spend Time Together

Shortly after Kaitlyn was born, I remember Larry coming home one day, looking around a room characterized by disarray, and voicing those six seemingly innocent words that strike terror in the heart of any stay-at-home mom. "So. What did you do today?"

After several weeks of unsuccessfully fielding this annoying question, I decided to answer it once and for all. I documented my activities, and when Larry came home that evening, I was ready for him.

"What did I do today? I changed nineteen diapers and played peekaboo seven times. I spent an accumulated total of ninety-seven minutes singing nursery rhymes and making animal noises. I washed one load of baby clothes and wiped spit-up out of my hair three times. I spent an accumulated total of four hours breastfeeding in that very recliner."

Time is a treasure, and the Bible tells us that where our treasure is, there our heart will be also. Where we invest our time, our heart will follow. Babies take time. Is it any wonder we love them?

When our babies are little, they chase us. Spending time with them isn't difficult. But when they're older, we may need to do the chasing! As our children mature, the demands on *their* time become more complex. At the same time my two-year-old was glued to my hip, my ten-year-old was busy with school and gymnastics and friends. Time together—time that's vital if we want to keep the loving feelings in our relationship—seems harder to come by as kids grow.

If we value our relationships with our kids, it's imperative to carve time out of busy schedules to be together.

Play, Don't Preach

When our children are toddlers, there's little use for formal instruction. The lectures, reprimands, and long-winded analyses that seem so indispensable when they're older don't have much impact during those Desitin years. So what do we do instead? We play. Remember Itsy Bitsy Spider, patty-cake, Five Little Monkeys, peekaboo?

As our kids mature, so does their comprehension. Suddenly we can communicate with them in so many other ways—we can lecture, instruct, chat, write notes, even shake a finger.

Unfortunately, in the process of gaining so many options, we sometimes abandon the form of communication that meant so much during those vital, formative years. What a mistake!

So play with your kids. Throw a ball. Wrestle in the snow. Stage ticklefests. Break out the board games. Buy some water guns and balloons and spend a hot Saturday afternoon cooling off. And whatever you do, don't be a martyr. Find an activity that is pleasing to both you and your child, and watch as your enjoyment of each other soars to new heights.

Give Undivided Attention

Have you ever tried to tell a baby, "I'll be with you in a minute, sweetie"? You and I both know that doesn't work. Babies demand our undivided attention. And if we don't give it to them—immediately—they scream at the top of their lungs until we do.

Of course, we don't allow that kind of behavior from our children once they're old enough to understand the concept of patience. And yet older kids need our undivided attention, too. They may have to wait five minutes or two hours until we've finished whatever it is we're doing, but once we turn our attention to them, they need to feel we're theirs and theirs alone.

What is the key ingredient of undivided attention? Eye contact. When our children are telling us about their day at school, lamenting a friendship gone sour, or explaining in painstaking detail the cool new video game a best friend just bought, it's tempting to nod now and then as we prepare dinner or fold laundry. But if we want to use the opportunity to really bond with our kids, looking them in the eyes and giving our undivided attention works wonders.

Reach Out and Touch Someone

If our relationships with our babies could be characterized by any one thing, it would be touch. Holding, feeding, dressing, and comforting a little one means physical contact. In fact, their survival depends on it!

As our babies grow, they gain mobility and independence. Before long, they get themselves through their day without much physical help from us. But when it comes to their emotional well-being, touch remains as important as ever! Make touch an important part of your relationship with your school-aged child or teen. Hug. Tickle. Hold her face in your hands as you tell her how much you love her. Wrap your arm through his as you trek across the parking lot after church. Even a pat on the back means a lot.

As kids grow, affectionate gestures from parents (especially in front of friends) can seem embarrassing. Tailor your affection so it doesn't traumatize your peer-conscious adolescent. But don't give up. Look for frequent, appropriate ways to share a touch with your child.

Cherish Your Children the Way They Are Today

We don't usually let our expectations for our babies' behavior get too far ahead of their development. In fact, we cherish those first few years, lamenting the passage of time.

Yet as our kids mature, we can become so caught up in pushing them toward more responsible adult behavior that we forget to cherish whatever stage they're currently in. We forget that thirteen-year-olds should not be expected to act like thirty-year-olds, no matter how much we beg, bribe, or cajole. We don't appreciate all the immaturity, silliness, and goofball behavior that goes along with being eight or ten or fifteen.

How then do we cherish our kids the way they are today? I often say to Kaitlyn, "Fourteen (or eleven or eight . . .) is such a wonderful age! Enjoy being fourteen, Kaitlyn; it's a great year!" Sometimes I ask her to tell me what it's like to be fourteen. What does she like the most? What doesn't she like? It's a great way to encourage communication, but it also serves as a reminder to me. These are precious, fleeting years I want to appreciate before they're gone forever.

When it comes to parenting, our commitment to our kids helps us plod through some of life's more stressful and distracting seasons. Our unfettered joy at the privilege of raising them helps us soar. Both are necessary. To think we can make it through years of parenting with all passion and no plodding is unrealistic. To think we can make it on sheer commitment and no romance is sad.

We already love our kids, but we can fall in love with them as well. They'll benefit, and we will too, because love heals. Passion energizes. And shared laughter fosters joy.

And that, if you ask me, is better than being grumpy any day of the week.

10

....

Be a Loser

Recently I joined a new gym. It's great, but I have one complaint. At my old gym, the scale was located in the women's locker room. At my new gym, the scale is right next to the front desk.

You know what this means, don't you? I can no longer engage in my normal pre-weighing ritual. I can no longer lighten my load by removing my shoes, socks, leggings, T-shirt, bra, panties, wedding ring, and all of my eye makeup before stepping onto the scale. It means I gain five pounds right off the bat.

I've always hated numbers—we've never had a good working relationship. Sometimes I think there's a conspiracy and that most of the numbers in my life are out to get me. This would include not only the numbers in my checkbook but the numbers on most watches and clocks as well.

But the ringleaders have got to be the numbers on my scale. They seem to have mean-spirited agendas all their own, especially that digit in the middle. The numbers on either side are okay—they can stay. It's that middle guy who is not only malicious, but stubborn to boot.

And of course, all three numbers are celebrating as we speak, because at my new gym they get to broadcast their mean-spirited agenda in a public setting. Just last week, for example, I was stepping off the scale when I commented to a woman standing nearby, "Not exactly the best news I've had all day!" She patted my arm. "Cheer up! At least your weight is lower than mine!"

As I was walking away the implication of her words began to dawn on me. How did she know my weight was lower than hers? She peeked! I can't blame her, though—how could she have done otherwise? It's hard to be discreet with my numbers celebrating maliciously the way they always do, with party favors and bottle rockets and raucous victory dances around the face of the scale.

Of course, there's always one solution. If I want to be able to go to my new gym, approach the front desk, and weigh myself without anyone taking notice of my weight, I can always resume my pre-weighing ritual.

A naked woman may not be discreet, but at least no one will be looking at the numbers on the scale.

Is Your Relationship with Food Adding to Your Pain?

I know we've all had bad hair days. I can handle those. But nothing makes me grumpy faster than a bad body day. Did I say "day"? Make that week. Or month. Or decade.

I've heard of women who say they're buxom and happy. They are overweight but have no desire to change their lifestyles or their waistlines. To these women I say, "More power to you."

But I know that my extra pounds put me in bondage. The hundred-plus pounds I gained were intrinsically connected to profound emotional pain, my addiction to food being both a symptom and a source of that pain. Bottom line? I was miserable.

What made me so miserable? Sure, it was the way I looked. At 250 pounds, there wasn't a photograph or an image in the mirror that reflected back to me the way that, in my heart of hearts, I truly wanted to look. But more than that, it was the way I felt physically: the lack of energy, the heartburn at night, the inability to find a comfortable position in which to sleep, the constriction of clothing that never seemed to fit quite right. Even simple things—like the fact that my legs were too big to cross under a table—were daily reminders that I was at odds with my own body.

But all of that paled in comparison to the misery generated by the way I felt emotionally. Every night I fell asleep vowing that tomorrow would be different, and every day I would break that promise to myself. I was in bondage, trapped by feelings of self-loathing. Even when I managed to break free for short periods of time, my nemesis always managed to shackle me once again.

Looking for a Magic Pill?

I have numerous friends who struggle with weight issues like I do. We laugh at the diet books that tell us that if we merely learn to eat carrot sticks instead of potato chips, we can be thin and svelte. If only it were that simple!

What about you? Is there something about your relationship with food and with your body that makes you grumpy? Are you being held hostage by an unwanted ten pounds or more? An unhealthy relationship with food may start as a response to other problems in our life, but eventually it can become a problem in its own right. Either way, it can make you feel defeated and out of control, trapped and in bondage.

About the same time my "dam" burst and pent-up emotional pain flooded my world, I decided to do something about my weight. This wouldn't solve the problems in my marriage, but it would help me to feel better about myself— and that certainly couldn't hurt! I think I've finally broken the chains during this past year. My war isn't over, but I'm winning the majority of my daily battles and I'm happy and encouraged. I've lost sixty pounds and have a goal of losing forty more.

As you can imagine, people come up to me all the time and ask how I'm doing it. Unfortunately, I can't give them the answer they're looking for, because they're usually hoping I've discovered some magic weight-loss secret. They want me to tell them that I take a miracle-producing weight-loss pill, or that I've learned all four verses of a potent weight-loss mantra, or that I've stumbled across a magic weight-loss cloth that, when I rub it all over my naked body at midnight under a full moon, causes me to lose fifteen pounds by morning.

But the truth is what we've all been hearing for years: Diet and exercise really do make a difference. (Okay, I did slip one "cheat" in there—a surgical procedure that accounts for ten of my sixty pounds. I'll tell you all about it in the last chapter, I promise!)

But a lot of what I've been doing boils down to diet and exercise.

Disappointing, isn't it?

On the other hand, maybe there is a little magic after all. Now that I think about it, there are indeed some juicy tidbits I can pass along, some road-tested tips that don't require counting calories or sweating like a horse.

What is the secret to my success? Diet? Certainly. Exercise? Without a doubt. But perhaps the real magic lies in the fact that during the past year, as I've wrestled with issues of emotional pain, I've also been examining my relationship with food. As a result, I've cultivated some brand-new perspectives that have made all the difference in the world.

Do you want to be a loser? Do you want to win the battle of the bulge? Are you tired of the way your relationship with food multiplies not only your dress size but your emotional pain as well?

Then let's see what we can do about it!

New Thoughts about an Old Problem

Here are eight insights that have the power to change your relationships with food and your body. Master these new ways of thinking, and changing your diet and your activity level will be far easier than you think!

1. Get Mad

I used to look in the mirror and feel sad. Last year I took a new approach: I got mad. I took a long, hard look at all the things my weight had cost me through the years—energy, sensuality, confidence, physical comfort, health, and more—and decided I'd had enough. We're often taught to control our anger, yet anger is a valid emotion and can be a tremendous motivator when given constructive outlets of expression. Get mad! Then use that anger to fuel a positive change in your life!

2. Identify the Benefits of Being Fat

I had put on so much weight, seemingly against my will, that I suspected that at some level I was reaping some sort of benefit from my weight. What could it possibly be?

I didn't have to think too hard. Even though I hated to admit it to myself, I knew. The feelings of disconnection in my marriage had rendered me lonely and vulnerable. Deep inside, I knew my weight was a way of protecting myself from illicit relationships, not because a big woman can't be sexy and attractive, but because when I binged, I buried my own sexual feelings so deeply there was no chance I would, or could, respond to anyone's advances.

A friend of mine gets a different benefit from being overweight. She is beginning to realize that she uses unwanted pounds to gauge how much she is loved by friends and family. She explains, "There's a little voice inside of me that asks,

'Will you still love me if I cut my hair? Or don't clean the kitchen? Or gain thirty-five pounds?'"

The fact is, unwanted pounds sometimes are a solution to a specific problem in our lives. I needed a way to protect myself from having an affair. My friend needed a way to test the devotion of those who loved her. Is there a problem you are managing to address with your unwanted pounds? Identify the problem, then begin to look for healthier solutions.

When I began my weight-loss journey last year, I recognized my problem and began looking for healthier solutions. I swore to myself, "I WILL NOT use fat as my ally anymore. I'll find another way to stay faithful. I'll fix my marriage or get counseling or find friends to hold me accountable. I don't have it solved yet, but I'll get working on it now so that by the time I need some healthy strategies, I'll have them in place. But, by George, I'm done clinging to these ugly pounds!"

3. Identify Your Enemy—and It's Not That Bag of M&Ms!

When one of my girlfriends decided to lose weight, I encouraged her in every way I could. Then, three days into her diet, I began to prepare her for failure.

"Lisa, the day will come when you blow your diet. You'll eat a half-dozen doughnuts or a bag of chips or the last spoonfuls of ice cream in the carton. It might happen today or two weeks from now. But it will happen. And when it does, I want you to remember this: The food is not your enemy. So you ate six doughnuts? So what? Over the course of a lifetime, six doughnuts will not make you fat. A bag of Doritos will not make you fat. A gallon of ice cream will not make you fat.

"Food is not your enemy. *Self-loathing is your enemy.*

"Because when you eat those things, you will be tempted to hate yourself. And it is the hatred—the feelings of guilt, shame, and loathing—that will drive you to consume another six doughnuts, another bag of chips, another gallon of ice cream, and eventually you'll manage to eat enough to pack on

102

the pounds. So when you blow your diet—and you will!—forget it and move on. Tell yourself, *Hey, I must have needed those doughnuts.* Don't give in to the *real* enemy."

One week later, Lisa called me on the phone. She said, "Karen, I have to admit, your 'self-loathing' speech kind of bugged me. I was bothered by the fact that you seemed so certain I would blow my diet. I thought you didn't have any faith in me! Even though I've started—and then failed—a hundred diets, I wanted to believe that *this* time things would be different. I wanted you to believe it, too.

"Then yesterday I scarfed down half a box of Cheese Nips. I started to feel really bad about myself, so bad that I figured I might as well eat some leftover cake to boot. Then I remembered your little speech, and it really made a difference. I decided not to loathe myself for those Cheese Nips—they weren't my enemy. And my compulsion to keep eating began to diminish."

Food is neutral. It's nothing. It can't hurt us. But when we are disgusted with ourselves, we sometimes use food as a weapon of punishment or control. If we can neutralize the *real* enemy—self-loathing—we'll probably discover that food has lost much of its power over us as well.

4. Train Your Schedule before You Train Your Body

When I began going to the gym, I was too out of shape to put my body through very rigorous training. But that was okay, because in order to achieve long-term success, the first thing I needed to do was spend time training my schedule.

In the past, every time I began a new exercise regimen, I punished my body mercilessly for a week, burned out, and then quit. This time I took a new approach. I told myself that, at least for awhile, my primary goal was merely to dress in my gym clothes, drive to the gym, and stand on the treadmill. Every day. Once I was there, if I walked for five minutes or fifty, that was great. But to meet my goal, the only thing I really needed to do was get there. Five days a week. No cheating.

This seemed doable. And so I dressed. I drove. I stood. And as long as I was there, I walked.

Of course, there were days that I groaned, "But I'm tired! I'm busy! I don't *want* to work out today!" But then I reminded myself of my very simple goal, so I got myself into my tennis shoes, into the car, and into the gym. There were a few days that I walked for ten minutes and went home. But most days I walked for twenty minutes. Then thirty. Then forty-five. Then I cranked up the speed. Then I jacked up the incline.

Before long I began experimenting with the Nautilus machines. When I started, I took the pin out of each machine. This meant that I wasn't lifting any weights, just the metal bar that holds the weights—that was all I could handle. I didn't punish my body, because I knew I'd be back the next day. My schedule was pretty disciplined by now. I had made exercise a priority. I never wondered, "Should I go to the gym today?" Instead, I made plans: "I'm going to the gym today. When shall I go?"

Six months into my program I worked out with a trainer for ten sessions. Jill Cowan introduced me to a foreign language that included words like bench press and biceps curls. Suddenly I was on the side of the gym with beefy guys in tank tops and muscled women in spandex. And guess what? I was holding my own, lifting weights and working hard and breathing deep and getting these really neat patches of sweat on the front of my shirt. (Actually, I was pretty excited about this. You see, I'd never been in good enough shape before to build up a decent sweat. My lungs and heart had always given out before I could get hot enough to sweat! So I was pretty jazzed at this development, although my enthusiasm over sweating has made some of my friends shake their heads and suggest that I try to get out of the house more often.)

Fast forward several months to the present.

Recently I was at the gym when a twenty-something mus-cled young buck approached me. Introducing himself, he smiled and said, "I don't usually go up to women and say this kind of thing, but I just had to let you know . . ." and he nodded appre-ciatively . . . "you've got a really great look going on here!"

Okay, so part of me is thinking that a REALLY spiritual woman wouldn't have been flattered by a compliment from a man half her age, but then the rest of me kicks in and says, "Get real! This is the best thing that has happened to me since discovering reading glasses!"

High five! A point scored for forty-something women everywhere!

So take heart. There's hope for us yet! We're never too far gone to feel healthy and confident about our bodies.

But don't put the cart before the horse—begin by training your schedule. Once you've got your schedule and your daily habits toeing the line, strengthening your heart and lungs, dropping pounds, toning muscles, and even turning a head now and then won't be far behind!

5. Throw Away Your Scale

In the past, I exercised with one goal in mind: to change those numbers on my scale. I would exercise for three days, search in vain for any sign of departing poundage, and then become discouraged and seek consolation at McDonald's.

When weight loss is our goal, we may have to exercise for weeks and even months before we see significant progress. This can be a real problem because—and I wish there was a way to say this gently!—you and I are *spoiled.* We're used to getting immediate results, whether we're talking fast food, faxes, FedEx, or e-mail. When you take a good look at our fast-lane society, you have to admit that we pretty much have the attention span of gnats.

Do we *really* want to exercise for months before we make progress toward our goals? No way.

So maybe we should change our goals.

I remember when I changed my goals. It dawned on me that I didn't have to exercise for weeks before acknowledging any results. Exercise has a whole list of benefits that are virtually immediate, but that aren't reflected on a scale. Within a day or two, I can experience increased energy, greater confidence, clearer thinking, enhanced agility, and boosted spirits. Within a week I can begin to enjoy the benefits of a stronger heart and healthier lungs.

So stop watching your scale and start listening to your body. When you think about walking around the block or driving to the gym, don't sigh defeatedly and say, "But why bother? I've got so much weight to lose, I'll never reach my goal."

Instead, say to yourself, "If I exercise today, I'll enjoy benefits *today*. I'll sleep better tonight, I'll feel better about myself, I'll have more energy, I'll have strengthened my heart and lungs, and I'll enjoy a sense of accomplishment. These are my goals, and they are achieveable. Today."

Enjoy these immediate benefits consistently over a period of weeks and months, and the numbers on your scale will begin to drop. Even if they don't, the daily benefits would be well worth the effort.

6. Practice "Fast Forward" Thinking

My friend Beth was at my house one night when she confessed a monster craving for Krispy Kreme doughnuts.

"There's a place over in Arlington that sells them," she said. "We could be there in twenty minutes."

I laughed. "Yeah, we could. But I'm trying to eat healthy this week. I don't want doughnuts."

"They're open late. It's not too late to go."

"Thanks for sharing. But I don't want doughnuts. And you told me you were back on your diet. You don't want doughnuts either."

"Actually, I think I do," she said mischievously. "If you won't come with me, I think I'll drive there myself."

I thought a moment. "Okay, close your eyes."

"Close my eyes?"

"Yeah. We're gong to play a little game. It's called Video Tape. Close them. Good. Now imagine a VCR. See all the buttons?"

"I see them."

"See the fast forward button? Push it."

She laughed. "Okay, pushing the button."

"Now run the tape forward to, oh, about an hour from now. You've just driven to Arlington, gone into the doughnut shop ..."

"Sounds good so far."

"... you've bought three doughnuts ..."

"Two. They're pretty rich."

"... you've just eaten both of them, and now you're back in your car, driving home. Tell me what you're feeling."

Beth was silent for a long moment. Then she said, "I feel like a failure. I feel defeated."

She opened her eyes. "Boy. Those doughnuts aren't doing a whole lot for me, are they?"

When cravings hit, ask yourself this simple question: "How will I feel twenty minutes after I've eaten this stuff?" If your answer isn't particularly pleasant, it's possible your craving will lose its power.

Fast forward the tape. Think past the food. You'll be surprised how empowered you'll feel.

7. Have Your Cake and Eat It, Too

That night, Beth and I continued to talk about how to have healthier relationships with food. At one point I said, "I know what a doughnut tastes like. I don't know, however, what it feels like to fit into that size twelve dress I just bought. I want to taste that *first*. Then, if I want to, I'll celebrate with a doughnut, maybe two."

I always figured I couldn't have my cake and wear a size twelve, too. But I'm not so sure. Maybe it's possible to have both—as long as I pursue them in the right order.

Do you want to treat yourself to new delights? Delights of health and fashion? Then do it. The food's not going anywhere. It'll be waiting for you when you're done. I haven't heard any reports that doughnuts are on the verge of extinction. The fact is, healthy eating doesn't mean abstaining from favorite foods forever, but just postponing the pleasure for a while to allow you to taste success in other areas of your life.

Someone once said, "Nothing tastes as good as thin feels."

I'm planning on finding out for myself.

Here's Not Looking at You, Kid!

About nine years ago I decided to start working out at my local gym. The problem was that I felt intimidated by all the hardbodies working out around me. I hated comparing my body to theirs, and I found myself wondering what they were thinking of me as well.

One day I left my glasses in the car. Blind as a bat, I stumbled victoriously into the gym. I say victoriously because suddenly all those spandex-clad tens with washboard abs were nothing more than colorful blurs. And when I pulled my sunglasses out of my gym bag and slipped them on, my defense was complete. I couldn't see them, and, behind my shades, I felt pretty invisible myself.

I no longer wear my Foster Grants to the gym. But they got me through a tough time. So you feel a litttle insecure? Intimidated? Been there, done that. The good news is that sometimes something as simple as a prop—sunglasses, a favorite sweatshirt, a Walkman playing favorite tunes—can ease us through the transition until our confidence kicks in.

8. Love Your Body—at Any Shape and Size!

Perhaps the most important lesson I've learned this year is that I can love my body at any shape and size. The numbers on my scale don't determine my worth as a woman. Indeed, when I weighed 135 pounds, I thought I had fat thighs and hated being seen in a bathing suit! Today, I weigh nearly 200 pounds and I feel stronger and sexier than ever before. I don't look like Cindy Crawford—but I'm realizing that I don't need to in order to enjoy my body.

My goal is not to be a perfect "ten." My goal is to stop abusing food, to gain strength, and to enjoy the way I look and feel. Centuries ago the psalmist wrote about the crafting of the human body, "We are fearfully and wonderfully made."

I couldn't agree more!

You Go, Girl!

I'd love to write an entire book on this topic. In fact, maybe I'll do just that. The pain that food has caused in my life—as well as the things I've learned this past year as I've gone about reclaiming my health and my figure—has made me passionate about this subject.

Will healthier attitudes about food and our bodies solve all the problems in our lives? No way. But when it comes to our relationships with food and with our bodies, we *can* feel confident and in control. We may even find ourselves feeling more confident about tackling and diffusing other sources of pain in our lives as well.

So come on! We can do this! In fact, if you're ever in Dallas, it would be fun to work out together. I'll get you a guest pass. We could meet up at my gym. You certainly won't have any problem recognizing me.

I'll be the woman near the front desk, standing on the scale. Naked.

11

....

Pain, Pain, Go Away . . .

There are a lot of things in my life I would LOVE to get rid of.

My memory isn't one of them.

Things That Elude Me

Unfortunately, my memory seems to be leaving me, which gives me empathy with whoever penned the phrase, "Of all the things I've lost, I miss my mind the most." Of course, I'm talking short-term memory here. My long-term memory is fine. This is why I can remember exactly how to hand-sign the name of my first big crush. (His name was Robert Greilach, and I spent hours sitting in math class, spelling his name in sign language under my desk. When I wasn't signing his name, I was wielding my eyelash curler in an adolescent ritual of puppy love, crimping my eyelashes fourteen times, one for each letter in his name. My heart survived the crush. My eyelashes weren't so lucky.)

So I can still sign the name "Robert Greilach" in my sleep, but I can't always remember why I've walked from one room to another. I can sing all seven verses of the *Gilligan's Island* theme song, but my daughter has to set an alarm to remind me to pick her up from school. I can recall with perfect clarity the paisley miniskirt and velvet choker I wore when I was thirteen, but I can never remember exactly where I've put my keys.

Actually, finding my keys isn't the problem that it used to be. This is because every Christmas my sister Michelle Willett buys me some high-tech, new fangled key-finder. I have a key-finder that is supposed to beep when I clap. I have one that glows in the dark. I have one with its own remote. To top it off, Kaitlyn gave me a flashlight for my key chain. Larry gave me a key chain pocket knife. Kacie gave me a stuffed Tigger key chain from a McDonald's Happy Meal.

So I haven't lost my keys in a long time. The key-finders never work for more than a week, but by now there are so many doodads on my key chain (or "the entertainment center" as Larry calls it) that I always know where it is. This is because it's really hard to misplace something the size of a toaster oven.

The other thing I can't seem to hang on to, besides my memory and my keys, is an ink pen. If you walked into my office this very minute, you would not be able to find a pen to save your life. One day the phone rang and I had to jot down the message with an eyebrow pencil. The strange truth is that if you want to find a pen in my house you have to walk upstairs to my bathroom. At any given time there are about twenty ink pens in the bathroom drawer, next to the tube of Crest. It took me a long time to figure out how my pens were migrating upstairs—then one day I realized that they were hitchhiking while tucked behind my ear. I stick them there while I work and forget about them until I'm getting ready for bed. Case closed. Mystery solved.

Things I'd Love to Lose

So my memory, keys, and pens elude me. Unfortunately, in an ironic twist of fate, my life is filled with other things I'd LOVE to lose but just can't seem to shake.

Unwanted pounds fall into this category, as do dust bunnies and grudges. A dozen stubborn chin hairs also make the list. (Electrolysis has helped the problem but hasn't solved it for good. I still shave between treatments. The good news is that I only look like George Clooney a couple times a month rather than daily. Too bad chin stubble on a woman can't be sexy. Double standards are *so* unfair!)

Something else that makes my list of things I'd love to lose are stubborn heart-hurts. You know the kind I'm talking about. Aches you can't seem to shake; they're with you when you go to bed and with you when you face the day. And they're not unlike American Express with an attitude because you can't leave home without them even if you try.

Bidding Farewell to Emotional Pain

But this book is about feeling better, so I figure there's *got* to be a way to say good-bye to emotional pain, for a day or a week, if not for a lifetime.

So how can we do it? How can we go about letting go of tenacious hurts, painful memories, and muscled grudges?

I wish the ideas I'm about to suggest were the final word on the matter. I wish I could, in three easy steps, hand you the solutions to all of your struggles. I can't. But what I can do is help you experience some milestones along the way. Here are some suggestions.

Take a Break

Sometimes taking even a temporary break from your pain can be beneficial.

I recently met a woman named Barb who told me this story.

Subjected to a series of brutal traumas in her lifetime—including being raped as a child—Barb had been living with profound emotional pain for many decades.

Recently she agreed to accompany a girlfriend on a week-end getaway, meeting up at a beach house in Florida. Two days before she was scheduled to fly from Dallas to Florida, she went to an appointment with a therapist she'd been seeing for several years.

This is what the good doc said to her: "I want you to take a *real* vacation. Not just from your family and work but from your pain as well. I want you to agree to leave your pain with me while you're gone. In fact, imagine handing it to me in a carefully wrapped bundle. I'll take good care of it while you're gone, and I promise you can retrieve it, right here in my office, when you get back."

Barb said the most amazing thing happened. She had a great time in Florida with her girlfriend. No flashbacks, night sweats, or panic attacks. Visualizing her pain being temporarily tended by someone else gave her a reprieve that helped revitalize her exhausted spirit.

If you're having a difficult time taking a break from your pain, solicit the help of a caring friend or professional. Hand over your pain for an hour, a day, or a week. If it sounds like a game, it's not, although I can assure you that if playing Candy Land or Pac Man would help us find healing for our wounded hearts, I'd recommend them in a New York minute. Bottom line: Try letting someone else take care of your pain for a while. After all, there's no dice to lose, and your foot won't fall asleep from sitting cross-legged in front of the TV with a video game control pad in your hands.

Find Symbols of Hope

Make a list of your hurts and burn it. Write yourself a letter. Plant a tree in your backyard. Write a poem. Take yourself out to dinner to celebrate a milestone in your healing. In other words, find something tangible that can be a symbol of hope as you loosen your grip on some of the pain you've been living with and begin moving toward wholeness.

For example, when one of my girlfriends was facing a challenge, she gained new heart when she saw an airborne sparrow struggle against the wind, climb to new heights, and finally begin to soar. Another friend who had lost her joy in life began collecting toy otters because they represented the playfulness she was ready to embrace in her own life.

One more example: Last year I attended a wonderful event at which sixty women came together for dinner and a speaker. It was an unusual evening, and what made it so unusual was the speaker. For starters, her entire name was Lemme. Just one name, sort of like Madonna or Cher.

But that's not what made Lemme, an art professor at Dallas Baptist University, so very memorable. Lemme is a potter, and after dinner she spent an hour with us, sitting at her potter's wheel, throwing clay and talking about women's lives and women's wounds and women's healing.

At one point during the hour, Lemme shocked us all by picking up a utility knife, placing it at the lip of the beautiful clay vase she was shaping, and slicing the vessel wide open from top to bottom. The clay immediately collapsed in her hands, its strength robbed by the massive wound. Sixty women gasped in unison.

Gently, Lemme began to repair the wound, knitting together the pieces and mending the broken place. The vessel spun countless times through her hands, and her strong fingers massaged the wound until what was once gaping was now just a crooked scar, a thin reminder of the trauma and the healing.

After the session, women crowded around a table where Lemme had arranged some of her pottery for sale. There was one sculpture that mesmerized us all. Called "The Potter's Hands," it depicted the scene we had just witnessed. There, in a pair of strong hands, lay a clay vessel, slit from top to bottom, gaping and wounded but on the threshold of a miracle.

Except the hands weren't meant to represent Lemme's hands. They were meant to depict the healing hands of God. And the clay vessel? There wasn't a woman in the room who wouldn't have been willing to say, "That wounded vessel is me." In fact, one woman had been crying cleansing tears all evening. Nursing a deep hurt from a divorce and the subsequent loss of her children, Sandra had been impacted by Lemme's message of hope. That night marked a milestone as she first embraced and then began to let go of some of her pain. And when she went home, she carried Lemme's arresting sculpture with her. Sandra told me she wanted it in her home to remind her, every day, that God had his hands on her wounds and that her healing was underway.

Letting go of our pain is a daily process, and sometimes it helps to have something we can look at—a specific event or a tangible symbol—to remind us of how very far we've come.

Pretend You're Normal

We've talked about taking a break and also about finding symbols of hope. If we want to give stress and pain the boot—if only for a couple of hours—we could always try something else: taking a temporary tour through the land of make-believe.

Look, I'll be the first person to say that TV is just pretend. (How else could every TV mom except Roseanne and Marge Simpson wear a size twelve?) But I think there's a way to use all that make-believe to our advantage.

One day my girls were squabbling so much that every word and deed seemed calculated to provoke and annoy. Finally I threw up my hands. I said, "Remember how last weekend we watched *Little Women* on TV? Remember how NICE those four sisters treated each other? Well, for one hour, I want you both to pretend you're one of the March girls. Kaitlyn, you're Meg, and Kacie, you're Amy. Ready? Set? Go!"

So I started thinking: If a little make-believe can banish bickering for an hour or two, why can't it get rid of grumpiness? Exile emotional pain? Deport depression? Don't misunderstand me—what I'm suggesting is hardly a long-term solution. It's an expedient measure at best, but sometimes a little short-term relief is just what the doctor ordered.

Think about how functional everyone seemed on *The Cosby Show*. Or how everyone in Mayberry looked out for each other. Or how optimistic the Bradys always seemed to be. What if you and I took a vacation from our lives and became, for the space of one hour, as "together" as Claire Huxtable, as nurturing as Aunt Bea, or as upbeat as Carol Brady?

Turn on the Tube, Borrow a 'Tude

What attitudes can we borrow from the TV women who have been visiting our homes for years? When we're stressed or in crisis, can we take a short break from our lives and make believe we're as healthy, confident, or forgiving as the following women, fictional though they may be? Let's tune in and borrow a 'tude for just an hour or two. Can we pretend to be . . .

as gentle as Caroline Ingalls
as "together" as Claire Huxtable
as forgiving as Wilma Flintstone
as emotionally intelligent as Annie Camden
as self-sufficient as Shirley Partridge
as playful as Jeannie
as competent as Samantha Stevens
as bubbly as Marion Cunningham
as gracious and strong as Florida Evans
as cool as Kelly, Sabrina, and Jill
as nurturing as Aunt Bea
as motivated as Elyse Keaton
as wise as Margaret Anderson

MANY THANKS TO TV TRIVIA TEAM KAITLYN LINAMEN,
CARRIE JONES, AND DARRELL PURDY

What's lacking in your life? Joy? Confidence? Optimism? Then take a hint from a TV chick and pretend you're brimming with what you're missing.

Understand the Benefits—and the Price—of Your Pain

In the last chapter I confessed that, when I couldn't lose weight, I was forced to say to myself about my unwanted pounds, "Since you keep hanging on to this stuff, you must be getting something in return. How might you possibly be benefiting from hanging on to this?"

When you and I can't seem to lose unwanted stress or pain, we might do well to ask ourselves the same question. If you're hanging on to painful emotions, do you know why? Understand the *benefits* of your pain.

I remember a time I was stressed and hurting so badly I couldn't think straight. A friend told me, "Karen, you're going to have to get rid of your anger at so-and-so. Not just for the sake of the person you're mad at, but for *your* sake—it's eating you alive!"

I said, "I can't. This has been a part of that relationship and a part of me for so long, if I let it go, what will be left?"

My hurt had become a significant part of my definition of that relationship. It was also starting to shape my definition of myself! Finally I viewed it as a way to protect myself from getting hurt again.

No wonder it was so hard to let it go!

In addition to understanding the benefits of your pain, I think it's also important to understand the *price* of your pain.

I think one of the reasons we might hang on to emotional pain is because we paid so much for it in the first place.

It's like the time I paid a couple hundred dollars for a down comforter. I'd slept under it a couple weeks when my allergies went berserk. My sinuses felt like the size of a Winnebago. My postnasal drip didn't need a doctor; it needed a plumber. I was miserable.

Did I get rid of the quilt?

Not on your life. I'd paid an outlandish price for that thing. How could I possibly get rid of something for which I'd paid so dearly?

Sometimes I feel that way about my emotional pain. Maybe it didn't cost me an arm and a leg, but it certainly cost me plenty in terms of joy and energy and happiness. How could I possibly get rid of something for which I have paid so dearly?

What have you paid? Barb, raped as a child, might say that the experience took her childhood and her innocence and handed her profound pain in return. Can she let go of something for which she paid such a heavy price? She may have to, if she's ever going to feel whole again.

I wish letting go of our pain was as simple as singing a revised version of the little ditty we all learned as kids:

> Pain, pain, go away...
> Don't come back another day!

Unfortunately, it's not that easy. The good news is that healing and wholeness are not beyond our grasp. I believe you and I can reach them, I really do.

So start working on losing that pain. I will, too.

That is, as soon as I finish looking for my keys.

P. S. Healing Images for Hurting Women

I have a number of friends who have experienced profound pain when as adults, they suddenly began remembering a traumatic event from their childhood. I have never experienced this kind of pain, but my heart grieves for women who have. When one of my girlfriends began experiencing this in her life, I wrote her the following letter. It talks about ways to relieve pain. It also describes some ways to visualize the therapeutic benefits of pain in our lives. She gave me permission to include the letter here. I hope it can encourage you or someone you know.

Marie—

I'm sorry you had a rough day yesterday. Yes, I know what it's like to feel lonely despite the fact that you are surrounded by people, and they're all laughing and talking, and you feel like you are outside looking in through a window, and you wonder if anyone can tell, if they can tell by looking at you how very far away and alone you are, even though you are right next to them in a crowded room.

I don't know why the memories can't stay submerged, I really don't. I mean, from your perspective and mine, that certainly doesn't seem like a bad plan. After all, they were forgotten, they weren't hurting anyone where they were, why not just leave them there? I don't understand God's ways, that's for sure.

Unless they were hurting you, where they were. Somehow, in some way, maybe in a way you weren't even completely aware of. Maybe, even though they were buried, they were manifesting themselves in some way that you never even associated with the memories. Maybe they've been hindering you in some way from loving fully, or trusting completely, or communicating in a healthy manner, or reaching out, or reaching in, or launching forward, or looking back, or handling stress, or parenting your kids, or something. And when all this is over, when you've come through these next months or years and you've got all these great insights and growth as a result, you'll look back and say, "Wow, I never realized how much those buried memories were crippling me in this way or that way."

It's something to think about, although I know it doesn't ease the pain at the moment. At this moment, very little will. At this moment, you're looking for life rafts, anything to keep you afloat for another day or hour or minute. Make a list, Marie, make a list of things that keep you afloat for just even a few minutes, and when you feel like you're coming out of your skin, go to that list. Pick something. Do it. And when it wears off, pick something else from the list. Over and over. All day long if you have to. E-mail someone. E-mail yourself. Play the piano. Lock yourself in the bathroom and cry. Grab a Walkman and praise tape (actually, rock and roll works best for me!) and go for a long walk by yourself. Make a collage out of magazine pictures. Make something out of Play-Doh, some shape that represents how you feel at the moment, or how you wish you felt. Crank up some upbeat music and haul your kids into the living room and dance with them. Organize a closet. Cry some more.

Get index cards and write out ten Bible verses that speak comfort and peace and healing to your soul. Tape them where you'll see them all day long—on the bathroom mirror, over the kitchen sink, by the computer. Dwell on the words. Memorize them. Make up little tunes and sing them to yourself.

I love you. There will be flowers and sunshine and breezes and laughter again in your life. I promise! Just hang in there, day by day, minute by minute. YOU WILL GET THROUGH THE MEMORIES AND THE PAIN. You WILL come out the other side. Until then, I know it's dark, I know it hurts, I know it feels like you're not going to make it, like you're going crazy even as we speak. But don't be afraid of the pain.

I remember going into the hospital to have my first baby. I hate pain. I'm afraid of pain. Pain always makes me think something terrible is happening to me. Pain makes me feel sort of panicky, actually.

Well, in the months before Kaitlyn was born, I worked hard to retrain my thoughts about pain. I told myself that some pain doesn't mean something is terribly wrong, it means things are going right. It means things are working the way they should, and the end result is going to be beautiful. The pain is a doorway. Actually, when you think about it, in childbirth, the pain is making a doorway through which something beautiful and alive and precious can come into your world.

Did those kinds of thoughts lessen the pain? Did they make labor and delivery hurt any less? Of course not. But they helped remove the panicky feeling. They helped me not to panic when I was really hurting.

Your pain means something is working as it should. Your mind and spirit are working the way they should, remembering the past trauma at an age and time when you are better prepared to deal with it.

And, like childbirth, this pain is creating a doorway through which God can bring new life and blessing and hope and joy and healing and wholeness into your life.

Now that I think about it, I guess childbirth is one image, but there's yet another image of pain that we might be able to benefit from.

Think about when your leg falls asleep. It's numb. No feeling. But when you begin to stretch and the blood begins to circulate again in that leg, it starts to tingle, then prickle, and suddenly the slightest movement can bring nearly excruciating jabs of pain, can't it? But the pain means that leg is coming back to life, being restored to its full feeling and function. And it hurts, and you're glad when it stops, but you certainly couldn't have functioned very well the rest of your life with a sleeping leg, could you? Imagine not being able to walk properly, stumbling, even being prone to injure yourself further because, with no feeling in your leg, you probably wouldn't have been as aware if you bumped or bruised or cut your leg.

Your spirit was numbed by whatever traumas you endured . . . and now God wants to restore feeling and function, but the pain is excruciating as blood rushes to those nerve endings and they start to wake up from their slumber.

Try to let go of the panic, Marie. This pain may well be a pathway to life and beauty, healing and wholeness, rejuvenation and renewal. Does knowing this make it hurt less? No way. But at least you know you're not going crazy. There's a purpose to this pain, a method to this madness. It's not random. It's not malicious or pernicious.

In the end—dare I say this? I dare, but only because I speak as someone who has just come through the most excruciating year of her own life, a year when pain threatened to overwhelm me completely and without mercy—in the end, perhaps we'll look back and see that the pain was, after all, our friend. That it took us on an unmerciful journey that, in the end, was merciful after all because it brought us to a better place, a place inaccessible except via the pain.

I'm still figuring it all out. I don't claim to have all the answers, or even some of them. I'm just still figuring it all out for myself. But I'm here for you, and cheering for you, and crying and grieving with you. So you feel alone, but you're not alone. You're loved and you are needed and you are precious and you are stronger than you think. Hang on.

Love,
Karen

12

....

Good Grief!

When Kaitlyn turned eleven, she wanted one thing and one thing only for her birthday.

Pet rats.

I didn't ask Larry what he thought about the idea. After all, there are just some things for which it's easier to obtain forgiveness than permission. Instead, I peeled open the Yellow Pages, looked under pets and, before you could say "mouse droppings," Cecelia and Megan had come to live with us.

They were adorable, all white and inquisitive and good-natured.

The little ladies had been a part of our family for about a week when I looked into their glass cage and noticed something tiny and pink wiggling next to Cecelia.

I blinked. Stared. Blinked again.

It was a baby rat.

I called the pet store.

The woman on the other end of the line sounded puzzled. "She must have been pregnant when she left here, although I didn't think either of those rats was near old enough. And I'm amazed there's only one baby. I've never heard of a rat giving birth to a litter of just one. Oh well. Think of it as a two-for-one special. Or maybe three-for-two. However you count 'em, congratulations and good luck."

Kacie, then two and a half, bonded immediately with the baby. Forget watching *Rugrats*—Kacie watched our own rats and daily monitored the progress of our tiny guest.

Everything was going great until one morning I looked into the nest and discovered that the baby rat had died during the night.

My biggest concern was how to tell Kacie. Larry and I discussed it at length. I voted for the straightforward approach, but Larry wondered if Kacie was too young to understand the idea of death, and in the end I agreed.

Telling It Like It Is

You know that old saying "what a tangled web we weave..."?

Well, I started weaving the very afternoon the baby rat died. After disposing of the tiny body, I pulled Kacie onto my lap and gently explained that the baby rat had simply "gone away."

This was my first mistake.

"Gone where? Who took it out of the cage? Does Cecelia know it's gone? Did it walk or go in a car? Where did it go? When is it coming back? Who's going to feed it while it's gone? Is it visiting its family? Is Cecelia sad the baby's gone? Can we go find the baby?"

I tried to answer all her questions. But in my attempt to protect her, I tried to answer her questions without actually giving her any accurate information. This, of course, led to more questions, and one thing led to another until ...

Two hours later, I called my mom in a panic. "I don't think I handled this very well," I explained. "I started off nice and vague, but Kacie bombarded me with so many questions that I guess I got a little carried away and now, well ... now she thinks the baby took a train to rat heaven. She's roaming the house yelling, 'Baby Rat, where are you?' trying to convince it to catch the 6:15 back home. This has gotten entirely out of hand."

When my mother responded, I could hear the smile in her voice. "Karen, it's simple. Here's what you need to do and say ..."

I followed her instructions to the letter.

My conversation with Kacie went without a hitch. I pulled the tiny body from the trash and let Kacie see and even touch the lifeless form (thank God for antibacterial soap!). I chose my words carefully when explaining how the baby had died. I didn't want to say the little rat had fallen asleep and would never wake up—what if Kacie became afraid to fall asleep herself? I didn't want to say the mother forgot to feed it—what if Kacie missed a meal and began to fear for her life? No, I had to pick a cause of death that had no easily identifiable counterpart in Kacie's world.

I told her the mother rat sat on the baby. I rarely, if ever, sit on my children, so this was probably a pretty safe choice.

I suggested we bury the baby in the backyard, but Kacie wasn't ready for that quite yet. It took three days of talking and looking and touching before she was ready to say good-bye. Then we took the baby rat into the backyard and buried it under a cedar tree.

This was Kacie's first encounter with death. But you and I know that death is an all-too-common part of life. Family members die. Friends die. Acquaintances die. Even pet rats die. Hopefully these deaths occur infrequently in our lives.

The truth is, though, that when you and I face death, it's much more likely to be the death of something intangible. But that doesn't necessarily make it less painful. On a regular basis, you and I face the death of things like relationships or dreams or even cherished parts of ourselves. When we're in deep pain, it often means we're hurting over the death of something that was important to us: love, hope, dreams, innocence, joy, friendship, and more.

It took me a while to realize that I wasn't just angry or sad or hurting over the wounds in my life—I was *grieving*. Looking back, I became excruciatingly aware of a massive number of small deaths that had gone unaddressed and unmourned in my marriage and in my own spirit. When the accumulation of these deaths became too much to bear, grief and pain crashed in on me with a vengeance.

Stages of Grief

Chances are you've heard folks talk about the five stages of grief. It makes sense that we go through these emotional stages when we've just experienced the death of a loved one. But we forget that we're just as likely to go through these exact same stages when we lose a job, have a best friend move far away, suffer the death of a marriage, lose our youthful bloom to advancing years, experience the violation of innocence or trust via betrayal or abuse, watch someone we love make destructive choices, or stand helplessly by while a dream crashes and burns.

What are the stages of grief? Well, we've already talked about one of them—*denial*—in a previous chapter. A different stage is *anger*. Still another stage is *depression*. Yet one more stage incudes things like *bargaining* or *blaming* as we give in to "if only" thinking such as: "If only I could make him love me again, I'm sure everything would be all right," or "If only I had been a better parent, I'm sure none of this would have happened." A fifth stage is *acceptance*. This is where joy and passion and purpose begin to flourish, and promising plans for the future begin to eclipse the pain of the past.

There's good news and bad news about grieving. The good news is that grieving is not unlike an arcade game. A pinball machine, to be precise.

The bad news is that we're the ball.

Grieving usually means ricocheting back and forth between denial, anger, depression, if-only thinking, and acceptance. Ping ping ping ping ping . . .

This has certainly been true in my life. In the past couple years, I've flirted with denial. I've wallowed in anger. I've wrestled with depression. I've blamed myself, others, even God.

Acceptance? I've had moments, and I'm keeping my fingers crossed for more of the same.

When you're in emotional pain, you may wonder why your emotions are all over the map. You may be too depressed to get out of bed one day and energized by fury the next. You may have moments of well-being and other moments when you'd give your right arm, your firstborn child, and your entire collection of Jan Karon novels just to be able to go back and undo some decision or event that landed you in the mess you're currently in.

Guess what?

You're normal.

You're grieving.

And while grief may be a pinball machine, eventually the ball will come to a rest. But while you're playing the game, learn the rules well. Pay attention to your emotions. Ask yourself what stage you're in today. Stay aware of your transitions back and forth and don't berate yourself for the inconsistencies in your feelings. Glean hope from the fact that "this, too, shall pass." But before it does, give yourself permission to do it all: Sleep. Cry. Rage. Pray. Analyze it ad nauseam.

When you feel unexpected moments of well-being, embrace them. Cherish them. Bask in them. Thank God for them. When they pass—because they will—and denial, anger, or depression well up in their place, don't despair, because the well-being will return. Next time it will last a little longer. And the next time longer still.

The ability to grieve, to grieve thoroughly and to grieve well, is a cornerstone of emotional wellness. It is a skill that we will need to call upon, not once or twice, but time and time and time again throughout our years on earth.

Out of the Mouths of Babes

Larry's grandmother died last year. When we heard the news, we packed up our van and drove from Texas to Arizona to be with other family members as we grieved the loss, remembered the legacy, and celebrated the life of Eyla Linamen.

Of course, this also meant I found myself with yet another opportunity to talk to Kacie about loss. Thankfully, Kacie was nearly four years old by now and had matured a little since our tiny pet took the train to rat heaven.

I thought about calling my mom again for advice. But Kacie wasn't the only one who had developed since the untimely passing of Baby Rat. I had learned a thing or two myself, and I was ready to handle this one on my own.

For just a heartbeat I wondered whether Kacie would be traumatized or comforted by viewing her great-grandmother's body. Then, remembering Cecelia's dear departed baby, Larry and I agreed that a straightforward, concrete approach was the best path.

We let Kacie view the body, which she found intriguing. Then I sat down with her on a sofa in the foyer of the funeral home and tried to explain what she had just observed. This is what I said:

"Kacie, yesterday you played all day, didn't you? You ran and played and got all dirty and messy. And at the end of the day, you needed to take a bath, so you went into your room, took off all your clothes, and ran naked into the bathroom. When that happened, you were in one room and your clothes were in another. Could your clothes run and play anymore? Could they move all by themselves? Of course not. They lay crumpled on the floor, worn and discarded, unable to stir or shift or move by themselves. But you weren't crumpled on the floor, were you? You were in the other room, naked, laughing and playing in the water.

"That's what happened to Great-Grandma. That's what will happen to all of us one day. Our bodies are like clothes. We wear them for awhile. We run and play, and after a while our bodies get wrinkled and worn. And when they're pretty much worn out, Jesus helps us to climb out of them. He lets us leave them crumpled on the floor, and we run on into heaven. That's where Great-Grandma is. Her body is here. But she's in heaven."

Kacie thought a moment. I knew I was in trouble when she said matter-of-factly, "So Great-Grandma is naked in heaven?"

"Yes, well . . ." I hedged. "I don't think she's still *naked*. I think God gave her another body to wear. You know, kind of like when you put on pajamas after your bath."

Kacie looked at her body and tugged at the skin on her arm. Then she looked at me. "How did Great-Grandma take off her body? I don't know how to take off my body. Can I climb out of my body, too?"

"Um, not exactly. We can't do it ourselves. Jesus has to help us. Only he knows when our bodies are worn enough and it's time for a new one."

"But how?"

"How?"

"How does Jesus do it?"

"Do what?" I was stalling for time.

"Get our bodies off us?"

I had no choice. I had to tell her.

That afternoon, Kacie ran to Larry's dad, climbed into his lap, and asked loudly, "Grandpa, did you know that God unzipped Great-Grandma's body? Grandma's body has an invisible zipper."

Dad blinked. "A zipper?"

"Yep. Everybody's does. We don't know where it is, so we can't unzip it ourselves. Only God knows about the zipper."

"I didn't know that."

"Yep. And do you know what happened then?"

"I can't say that I do."

Kacie's eyes widened with excitement as she leaned in close and blurted, "Great-Grandma ran naked into heaven!"

Perhaps I should have called my mother for advice after all.

Life after Death?

Most of us are pretty comfortable with the idea that when a loved one dies it isn't really "the end" but a new beginning. We accept the idea that physical death is a doorway into a new kind of life, a life in eternity.

This same principle applies to other kinds of death as well.

For example, flowers die. As they die, seeds fall and germinate into new growth and new blooms.

Creatures die. Their bodies return to the soil, creating fertile ground for vegetation that will feed and shelter a new generation of wildlife.

Dreams die. And yet, even as we sift through the ashes of one dream, we often find the stirrings of hope for another.

As we're hurting and grieving—bouncing like pinballs between denial, anger, depression, if-only thinking, and acceptance—it may not be possible to cheer ourselves up with the idea that this pain may very well be a pathway to new joy, new hope, new beginnings, new life.

But the fact that we may not be able to fully grasp this principle doesn't mean that it's not true.

Want to Grieve Well? Then Keep on Truckin'!

My friend Beth is a nurse. My friend Darrell has been disfigured since birth. I figured they were both qualified to talk about grief, Beth from a clinical perspective, and Darrell from a personal perspective, because he grieves the loss of things he's convinced he may never experience because of the way he looks.

I asked each of them to tell me what they've learned about grieving, and they both agreed that grief is a process by which we get from one place to another.

Darrell put it this way—grief isn't usually about an ending as much as it's about a transition. He said, "I grieve over my appearance. Because of the way I look, I don't get to manage my emotional and social needs in the traditional ways. But that doesn't mean I just lose hope and wait to die. It means, however, that I have to work hard to find alternative ways of getting those needs met."

He added, "Here's another example. If my mom died tomorrow, I might be tempted to think that my relationship with her was over. But in some fashion, my relationship with her would continue through memories, conversation with other people who loved her, photographs, meaningful rituals like buying her favorite flowers on her birthday, or whatever. Harnessing the power of grief helps me to make that transition between how I *want* things to be, and how they *can* be."

Beth says that there's yet another way in which grief is like a journey, pointing out that unhealthy grief is a pathway to despair, while healthy grieving leads to hope.

And if you want to take the pathway to hope, the key is simple:

Keep moving.

Beth explained, "As you bounce back and forth between the five stages of grief, there will be times when you don't want to talk about your loss, or when you can't concentrate, or when you feel immobilized. But if you get stuck in any one stage— if you just can't seem to move past denial, or anger, or depression—then that's not healthy grieving and you might want to talk to a professional who can help you get unstuck."

So grief is a transition. A journey. In fact, the words "road trip" come to mind, which makes me wonder how I should pack in order to keep those wheels turning. If I were driving from Dallas to Denver, my packing list would include my gas card, cell phone, a change of clothes, a grocery bag of snacks, a cool pair of shades, and my collection of Shania Twain tapes. But if I want my grief to transport me effectively from pain to hope, how can I pack? What's on the list? A box of Kleenex comes to mind, as does a comfortable pair of shoes for long, reflective walks. How about a journal in which to arrange my deepest thoughts? Not to mention the phone numbers of close friends, family, and maybe even a pastor or therapist. Finally,

I think I'd want to pack a calendar instead of a watch, because I'll probably be measuring my progress over weeks and months instead of minutes and hours. But even though grieving takes time, it's time well spent, because there's just not an alternate route that will get me where I want to go.

Getting from one emotional state to another *is* possible.

And healthy grieving is the road that gets me there.

13

....

Girls Just Wanna Have Fun

bout eight months ago I was working in my kitchen when a bizarre thought popped into my head. I usually ignore these thoughts, attributing them to a juvenile attempt to distract myself from unpleasant tasks at hand, which on that particular day happened to be excavating my Corning Ware from under several layers of baked-on crud and emptying the crumb catcher on my toaster (harvesting croutons for that night's salad, if I'm not mistaken).

But that day was different—I didn't shrug off the idea that popped unbidden into my head. Instead, I laughed out loud and said, "Well, why not?" I went to the Yellow Pages, made a few phone calls, and it was a done deal.

I was so excited, I just had to tell someone.

I called my folks. My dad answered the phone.

"Guess what?" I blurted. "I just signed up for belly dancing lessons."

He laughed. His laugh had this sort of *kids-these-days, what-are-you-gonna-do* ring to it, even though his "kid" is just a few years shy of menopause. He hollered away from the phone, "Geri, you'll never guess what your daughter is up to this time.

She's going to . . . I can't even say it. I'm going to let her tell you herself."

My mom got on the line, and I told her my news. She asked what had prompted this new passion. I said it would be great exercise, but that mostly it just sounded like fun. My dad wondered where I was intending to use my new skill, and my mom added, "NO belly dancing at restaurants or men's clubs." That seemed like a reasonable request. My mom said if she lived closer she'd take lessons with me.

I began my lessons the following week. They turned out to be even more fun than I thought they would be. I have my own finger cymbals—actually, they're called zils—and I even bought a pair of harem pants. You won't see me shimmying at any Moroccan restaurants, but I'm having a blast. (And apparently I'm not the only one—when I mentioned this experience in the humor column I write for the Women of Faith web site, I got lots of responses from women who have discovered the same brand of fun! Some women are looking for exercise, others for something fun and wacky to do with their girlfriends, but regardless of motive or means, they all gave me basically the same advice: "You go, girl!")

Although it was great discovering the correct way to do a shoulder shimmy, the best part of the experience was rediscovering how to have fun. Belly dancing was for me, well . . . playful.

And I hadn't felt playful in a long, long time.

Fractured Funny Bone

In the past couple of years, I've experienced some dark times when I felt overwhelmed by the stress and hurts in my life. I wasn't living *with* Grumpy, I *was* Grumpy. And whenever I feel like that, one of the very first things to go is my penchant for playfulness. Being playful requires things like lowering my guard, enjoying the moment, and not taking myself too seriously, and when I'm hurting, stressed, or grumpy, those things are far easier said than done.

I remember one day a friend of mine asked to see some old photos of me. I thought it was an odd request, but I complied, digging out some snapshots from my twenties and early thirties. I was curious to see what point he was trying to make.

He didn't waste any time in making it. He said, "Look at your face in these photos. You've always had this sort of happy, bubbly demeanor. But lately you just look miserable. You've lost your glow."

I figured my glow might be lost, but at least it wasn't lonely. Wherever it had gone, it was accompanied by my creative bent, my playful streak, and my sense of humor. I hoped they were having fun, because I certainly wasn't.

As I began to work to alleviate my stress, manage my pain, and pursue some healing, a funny thing happened. I started feeling mischievous. Then playful. Eventually I even began to experience some moments of joy.

Some folks may have shaken their heads at my belly dancing adventure, but the truth is, the rediscovery of my playful side was a good sign. I was feeling better. What's more, my playfulness was both a result and a catalyst of my healing. If you put a mirror next to a candle, that mirror not only reflects the light, it doubles the light. That's what happened to me. My playfulness not only reflected the healing that was going on inside of me, it doubled that healing, moving me even closer to health and wholeness.

Which means I saved a lot of money. Psychotherapy can cost hundreds of dollars.

Zils cost less than twelve.

Having Fun Is Serious Business

Remember when we were kids and something as simple as a game of Twister could make us laugh until we needed CPR? It didn't take much to tap into our creative, playful sides. But as we matured, stress, responsibilities, and emotional pain often robbed us of these childlike qualities. But it doesn't have to be this way. We *can* feel playful, creative, and spontaneous again. We *can* double our delight, multiply our merriment, and jumpstart our joy.

I'll be the first to admit that incorporating more fun into your life isn't going to solve even half of your problems. But it won't hurt anything—in fact, it may even promote healing in your life. Here are some ways to make it happen.

Fill in the blank. Wanna have more fun? It might be easier than you think. Let's start by filling in the blank of the following sentence:

"I've always thought it would be fun to_____."

Beth says she's always thought it would be fun to grab several girlfriends and take a road trip from Dallas to Memphis. The mission would be to return to Dallas with the tackiest Elvis souvenir they could find. She's already talked me into the trip and is looking for two more volunteers. If you're interested, holler.

Monique Robbins says she's always thought it would be fun to skydive. She speaks in rapturous tones of the ultimate thrill, the adrenaline high, the absolute rush. I asked her if she was talking about the rush of the wind whipping up her nostrils, but she said I shouldn't knock it till I tried it. I protested that I'd be so scared I'd probably wet my pants. She assured me that, even if I did, what with the wind velocity and all, they'd be dry in no time.

Jeanette Bassett says that she's always thought it was great fun to get up in the middle of the night and go out for little escapades. Recently she and husband David got up at 2:00 in the morning and drove to IHOP. They shared nachos and sausage and eggs and strawberries with whipped cream (and Rolaids?). In the future, she'd love to host a slumber party for a handful of close girlfriends. No husbands, no kids, just exchanging beauty tips and intimate secrets and eating junk food into the wee hours of the morning.

When we're stressed or depressed, fun often feels out of reach. Even if we think of something that sounds like fun, we tend to nix the idea, thinking, "I can't take time to do that," or "It's too much trouble."

But fun is a lot more accessible than we think. For Beth it's as close as her car keys. For Jeanette it's as close as a local restaurant. For me it was as close as the phone book. For Monique it's as close as . . . well, Monique may have to reach a little farther, as in fourteen thousand feet above ground level. But basically, fun is attainable.

I know you're busy. I know you're stressed. And, of course, financial considerations and moral boundaries come into play as well. But this isn't rocket science. "I've always thought it would be fun to_____." Fill in the blank. Life's too short not to have some fun.

Play a practical joke. My friend Jerry Spurlock, an airline pilot, told me the story of a buddy of his who was flying for a major airline. One day, in the middle of the flight, this captain left the cockpit and, holding two ropes in his hands, began backing down the center aisle of the plane. Every eye in the cabin was riveted to him as he backed up to a little old lady sitting next to the aisle. He asked if she would hold the ropes and, bewildered, she agreed. He thanked her, explaining, "I'll just be a minute. I have to use the rest room and I need someone to steer the plane."

There's nothing like the great feeling that comes from executing a successful practical joke. Pulling off a practical joke is therapeutic for several reasons. For starters, humor in any form is healing. Then there's the fact that practical jokes get our creative juices flowing, which not only feels great but means the pump is primed if we decide to apply those same creative juices to solving the problems in our lives.

But if you're like me, when you're stressed or hurting it's not always easy to give rein to your playful side. Wouldn't it be great if we could look for more playful ways to relate to folks around us?

A while back I took my kids to spend a week in Colorado visiting my parents. My sister Renee, her husband, Harald, and their boys planned a visit at the same time.

Late one afternoon I realized I needed something from the market. Harald and Renee had gone jogging, so I left the kids with my mom and headed for the store. I was heading down the gravel road that leads from my parents' house to the main thoroughfare when I spotted my brother-in-law's green T-shirt draped across a bush on the side of the road. Pulling over, I snagged the shirt and then roared on down the road, in a hurry to finish my shopping and get home before the joggers returned.

I didn't know what I was going to do with Harald's shirt, but I knew it had to be good.

When I got home from the store, I dropped the groceries on the counter and hollered for the kids to come help me. We quickly brainstormed about how to turn Harald's shirt into a scarecrow of sorts, then ran around the house looking for supplies to turn our dream into reality. We stuck a broomstick in a lawn chair, the weave of the fabric holding the straw bristles straight up in the air. Draping Harald's shirt over the bristles, we added a paper plate head, Play-Doh face, and yardstick arms. We planted our new friend on the backyard deck and waited for Harald to come home.

Harald was home for twenty minutes before the figure on the deck caught his attention. He swiveled his head in a double take, then burst into laughter. His reaction was great, but it wasn't the thing that made the joke so memorable. No, the part I'll always remember is the bright-eyed energy, the pell-mell scurrying, the let-it-rip laughter, and the creative synergy I got to experience with my two daughters and three nephews as our practical joke took shape.

Getting playful is good. Getting creatively playful is even better.

Don't act your age. When was the last time you swung so high you touched the sky with your toes? Or spun in circles till you collapsed on the grass? Or squeezed into a kiddie ride at an amusement park?

If you happen to be my dad, the answer—at least to the last question—is a few months ago. That's when he accompanied my mom, my two daughters, and me to Santa's Workshop, a Christmas-themed amusement park just outside of Colorado Springs.

My dad started out doing the normal grandpa sort of thing—you know, walking sedately, handing out quarters, taking pictures. But when Kacie hesitated to join other kids her size on a flying reindeer ride, the kid in my dad took over.

"Will that thing hold me?" he asked the ride attendant, gesturing toward the tiny reindeer-shaped car that would soon be airborne, spinning around the base of a forty-foot metal Christmas tree.

The teenager manning the controls shrugged and said "Sure," (like he knew), and my dad launched forward with a grin. "Com'on, Kacie," he said, and she ran ahead of him, snagging the blue reindeer while my dad nabbed the red.

I don't know who had more fun, Kacie and my dad, the rest of the family as we watched and snapped photos, or the dozen total strangers who gathered to smile and wave at the silver-haired occupant of the red reindeer car. All I know is that as my dad unfolded himself from his seat, he got a couple of thumbs-up. And as we were leaving, we passed a young boy trying to drag his forty-something dad onto the ride with him. After looking at us, the dad grinned, shrugged, and let his son pull him through the gate.

The number of our birthdays may be determined by the seasons, but our age is up to us.

Play is healing. It leaves us relaxed and rejuvenated. It makes us smile. It exercises our creative muscles. Play can even make us feel less isolated, because we're most often playful in the company of other folks.

No matter what we're wading through—a shallow stream of trivial stresses, or deep currents of serious hurts—we serve ourselves well when we lighten up and exercise the power of play.

The finger cymbals are optional.

14

Love Your Scars

Earlier in the book I told you that I have managed to lose sixty pounds. I also hinted that, halfway through the experience, I decided I needed a helping hand.

I wanted to lose weight the sane way, through diet and exercise. At the same time, I knew I had abused my body for so long that my misshapen tummy wasn't going to just snap back into shape as the pounds disappeared. I had recently signed a book contract and had a check on the way, so I picked up the phone and made an appointment to see a doctor.

I explained my problem to him like this: "I have this sort of apron thing going on. I can't take it off when I leave the kitchen. It won't go away when I lose weight. The best I can hope for is that when I'm done dieting it will be a *thin* apron. But it's always going to be there, forever and ever, unless you can help me."

He agreed to do just that. Six weeks later, I had a tummy tuck and shed ten pounds in two hours.

I didn't wake up thin, but at least I woke up with a proportionate body. For the first time in a decade my hope soared. This was the break I needed! Suddenly I knew that with continued healthy eating and exercise I could go all the way. I could have a healthier, stronger, shapelier body!

So I woke up feeling hopeful. I also woke up wrapped in a Velcro girdle thingamajig to keep the swelling down.

On my third day home from the hospital I felt brave enough to unhook the Velcro and peel away the abdominal binder so I could sneak a peek at my body.

I looked in the mirror.

My heart didn't just skip a beat; it dropped to somewhere in the vicinity of my left kneecap. I had read in a pamphlet that the incision would be long—hipbone to hipbone. I had no idea it would be *this* long.

I rewrapped my body and, fighting a simmering panic, wandered into the den where Larry was watching TV.

"I looked at the incision," I blurted.

Larry said, "Are you upset about it?"

I answered, "I might be. I'm still deciding."

The truth is, I felt confused, and a little betrayed. I was still sorting out my feelings half an hour later when I returned to the bathroom, locked the door, and undressed slowly.

I stared at myself in the mirror.

The incision was very symmetrical. It started high at one hip, swung south in a gentle arc, then headed north past the other hip. I figured bikinis were out of the question (as if that question had even been asked!). But sexy French-cut one-piece suits that rode high on the hip were a real possibility.

As I looked and evaluated, I asked myself, *Do I want to give back this incision in return for the shape I used to have, a shape I hated?*

The answer was no. Then it dawned on me that the scar that would one day replace my incision would be, well, like a badge of courage. I had wanted something for myself, and I had made it happen. It required time and money and courage; it involved pain pills and blood and indignities. But I had done it, and the scar would be my proof.

I decided that I wasn't going to hate my scar. I wasn't going to avoid it or feel embarrassed by it or wish it were gone. I was going to love it.

Running my hand gently along my belly, I made a promise to myself.

Whenever I stand in front of a mirror and view my scar, I'm not going to see a flaw. I will see a smile. A happy curve. A generous grin.

And I'm going to smile back.

Assigning New Meanings to Old Wounds

I've kept that promise to myself. My scar is beautiful. It says things about me that I appreciate. It says I'm not perfect. It says I've struggled and made mistakes. It says I persevered and reclaimed a part of my life I had lost. It also says I got a second chance, and for that I am profoundly grateful.

Sometimes I think it has been easier to deal with that scar than with the other scars in my life, the ones not inflicted with a scalpel but with choices and words and deeds, my own and those of others around me. To tell the truth, for every bodily scar, I have dozens of emotional scars. And I'm not alone! My guess is that you've got 'em too.

When we look at our hearts and see those inevitable dings and scratches, scars and flaws, weaknesses and broken places, do we feel grumpy? Or grateful? Do we feel shame? Or self-respect?

When I found a new way to think about my fleshly scar, I turned my back on shame and embraced self-respect instead. When it comes to our emotional scars, can we find a way to do the same? Can we look beyond the ugliness and see the beauty?

I think there's a way to do this; unfortunately, I'm still figuring out just what it might be. I still think about many of my scars, flaws, and weaknesses, and find myself crippled by a flood of negative thoughts and emotions.

But let me share with you a few of my thoughts on the matter. Is it possible to love ourselves in spite—and maybe even because—of our scars? Is it possible to look at things in our lives that could very well have left us diminished, depressed, or destroyed . . . and glean strength and hope and character instead? In the paragraphs below you'll find four affirmations. If you and I could take them to heart, perhaps we could begin to find the courage to love our scars.

Affirmation #1: I Am Real.

Remember Margcry Williams' classic story *The Velveteen Rabbit?* The Velveteen Rabbit was a stuffed bunny, the favorite plaything of a little boy who loved him very much.

Unfortunately, in the process of being loved, this rabbit got rained on and dragged around. He got bruised and torn, muddy and worn. But that love—even though it sometimes hurt—was the thing that made him *real.*

The wise old Skin Horse in the nursery explained it well:

> "Real isn't how you are made. It's a thing that happens to you. When a child loves you for a long, long time, not just to play with, but REALLY loves you, then you become Real."
>
> "Does it hurt?" asked the Rabbit.
>
> "Sometimes," said the Skin Horse, for he was always truthful. . . . "Generally, by the time you are Real, most of your hair has been loved off, and your eyes drop out and you get loose in the joints and very shabby."

Wouldn't it be great if there were an easier way? But the truth is that you and I love imperfectly, the people who love us love imperfectly, and sometimes we hurt each other in the process. We have scars and patches and threadbare places, and there are days when we feel as if we're coming apart at the seams.

Loving and being loved exacts a toll. But love is also a profound privilege, because you and I have the opportunity to discover what it means to be fully human.

We have the chance to become Real.

Affirmation #2: I'm Stronger Than I Thought I Was.

Sometimes, however, our wounds are not inflicted by the flawed nature of human love. Sometimes they are the result of random, tragic things that happen to us.

Two years ago I took a look at my emotional scars and said, "I feel as though I'm never going to be whole again. I'm so much more broken than I ever thought I'd be!"

In the past six months I've been wondering if there's a healthier way to look at those scars. Could I look at my scars and say, "Wow, look what I've survived! I'm stronger than I thought I was! I wish I hadn't suffered, but since I did, I'm not going to overlook the fact that I'm deeper and wiser and stronger as a result."

Sometimes life's not fair. And yet, like diamonds showcased on black velvet, our strength and mettle often shine against the backdrop of injustice and tragedy.

If your scars could talk, what would they say about you?

Would they say that you are broken beyond repair?

Or would they say that you have strength and depth beyond your years?

Affirmation #3: I'm Not Perfect.

Sometimes our scars are a result of our own sinful nature, and these often can be the most difficult to deal with.

When Kaitlyn was little, I worked hard to build her self-esteem. I read all the pop psychology books. I knew all the terminology. I told her she was great and perfect and special and smart and wise and loved. I told her that even when her choices were bad, *she* was inherently good.

So when Kaitlyn was about eight and experienced a month when all she could do was cry and say how *bad* she felt inside, I was at a loss. I thought, "Where did I go wrong? I've spent nearly a decade building this kid up, and now she says she's a horrible person. I don't get it."

I continued telling her how great she was.

She still sulked.

I continued telling her she was perfect and good.

She didn't buy it.

Then one day it dawned on me why she was having a hard time believing me—I wasn't telling her the whole truth.

That night, sitting on the edge of her bed as I tucked her in, I 'fessed up. "Kaitlyn, you're right," I said. "The truth is, you *are* bad."

She blinked a couple of times. "Really?" she said.

"Really. I meant all the stuff I said about how you're special and loved and precious and wonderful. Every word of that is true. But this other thing you feel is true, too. You may be precious, but you are not perfect. There's a part in you—a part in all of us—that is broken and rebellious and capable of great evil. That's what you're feeling right now. You're growing up, and you're realizing that you can be pretty selfish and rotten."

For the first time in several weeks, she smiled. "Yeah," she said, and there was a note of relief in her voice.

"Kaitlyn, you've discovered the secret."

"The secret?"

"You, me, Dad, Kacie—in fact, every single person in the world—we're not perfect or righteous or even good. We're always going to fall short. Always have times when we make mistakes. Get selfish. Act mean. Feel rebellious."

"Yeah?"

"Yeah. And that's why we need Jesus."

What pop psychology tells us is flattering. Pop psychology tells us that we're all okay—but the Bible says "NOT!" The Bible refers to something called a "sin nature," which is just another way of describing exactly what Kaitlyn was feeling. It says we're filled with all sorts of lusts and rebellion; it says we're selfish and capable of every sort of evil under the sun.

But if you ask me, what the Bible says is a relief, because it lines up more with my personal reality. I know there is sin in me, and sometimes this inner ugliness leads me into choices and actions that not only leave me wounded and scarred but leave folks around me wounded and scarred as well. When this happens, I'm tempted to give in to panic and shame, saying to myself, "You monster! Worm! Lowlife! You're defective, broken, and unacceptable. You should be ashamed of yourself!"

But I'm learning instead to realize that sinfulness is a problem everyone wrestles with. I'm learning to admit my shortcomings and acknowledge my need for a helping hand from a loving Savior.

My "sin nature" may leave me humbled.

It doesn't have to leave me shamed.

Affirmation #4: I Am Loved.

"I'm real."

"I'm stronger than I thought."

"I'm imperfect."

Here's the last one, and it's actually the best of the bunch. It's simply this: "I am loved."

Friend and psychologist John Smeltzer says that to feel loved despite the fact that we are ordinary, weak, and sinful is one of the truly greatest gifts we can receive. And there's only one Person who can love us like that. Unlike earthly family, friends, and lovers, this Person loves us with a perfect love that doesn't ever leave us wounded or empty. In fact, his love heals and satisfies like nothing we've known before.

I'm talking about Jesus.

Jesus doesn't freak out over our scars. He isn't frightened by our anger or our shortcomings. He isn't bewildered by our emotional pain, put off by our doubts, disappointed by our depression, or overwhelmed by the chaos in our hearts and lives.

There's a Scripture passage I've always loved, and it's this one: "Who shall separate us from the love of Christ? shall tribulation, or distress, or persecution, or famine, or nakedness, or peril, or sword? . . . For I am persuaded that neither death, nor life, nor angels, nor principalities, nor powers, nor things present, nor things to come, nor height, nor depth, nor any other creature, shall be able to separate us from the love of God, which is in Christ Jesus our Lord" (Romans 8:35, 38–39).

This profound love is amazing not only in its tenacity, but also in what it manages to accomplish. This is because the love of Jesus fills in all that empty space, the yawning chasm that exists between little ol' imperfect me and a perfect God.

The Bible tells the story of a wayward son who left the comforts of home for the seductions of the world and ended up broken and hopeless on the streets. He made a decision to go home, but before he could get there, his loving dad spotted him and ran—actually sprinted—toward the boy. The love of Jesus does exactly that. It sprints toward us, closes the distance, brings us into contact with our heavenly Father. Suddenly we're embraced in a bear hug and God whispers in our ear, "Welcome home."

I've met folks who have said, "But I'm too angry for Jesus to love me," or "My life is too messed up for God to help me," or "I've made too many mistakes. I'm sure he wants nothing to do with me now."

I have one word for them, and I think it's theologically sound. Poppycock.

We Can't Get Too Grumpy for God

Sometimes it's the little things in life that make me grumpy. It's the fact that I set a dish towel on fire, or ran over my cell phone with my van, or dropped my car keys in the commode. It's the fact that my hair keeps leaving my head and showing up on my chin.

But sometimes the pain is deeper, isn't it? It's in a marriage that isn't working or in the heartache that comes when our kids rebel. It's in the loss of a job or a relationship, or in our own souls as we struggle with depression or addiction. We feel it when illness strikes close to home, in our lives or in the life of someone we love.

Sometimes I feel overwhelmed by the chaos, brokenness, and scars in my life. And then I do something silly—I jump to the conclusion that if these things are overwhelming to me, they must be overwhelming to God.

But let's think about that a moment.

Is God stymied by chaos? I don't think so. I mean, we're talking about Someone who uses chaos the way you and I use modeling clay. After all, he took the chaos of a formless void and crafted the heavens and the earth, darkness and light, land and sea, stars and moon, fish and birds and creeping things, and even man and woman.

Or is God bewildered at the brokenness in our lives? Not really. In fact, I'm learning that he specializes in using broken things. I know this because he took the broken body of his Son, Jesus, and with it purchased hope and healing and salvation for generations of folks, you and me included. All we have to do is say, "Yes, Jesus, I receive all that you made possible for me to receive, through your death on the cross." And he takes our broken hearts and wounded spirits, and into these humble vessels he pours his precious Holy Spirit.

Finally, is God embarrassed by the scars in our lives? Does he avert his eyes? Does he love us less because our psyches bear the disfiguring marks of the mistakes of others and our own mistakes as well? Not on your life. Not when his own Son has scars on his hands and feet, face and body. Not when Jesus was wounded for our mistakes and bruised for our rebellion.

Not when it is by his very scars that we are healed.

Still Laughing After All These Tears

About eighteen months ago, when I was smack dab in the middle of some of the worst of my pain, I was traveling on business and got to spend several days with my parents.

An hour before leaving for the airport to return home, I was in the den packing up my stuff and chatting with my folks when my mom took a deep breath and said, "I had a dream about you a couple months ago."

I was immediately interested. Sometimes my mom taps into really intuitive, fascinating stuff in her dreams—sometimes they even come true. I said, "Dream? About me? What was it?"

She winced. "I wasn't going to tell you."

Now I was *really* intrigued. "But now you're going to, right? Because I really want to know."

She nodded slowly, then said, "Okay, here it is. In my dream, I saw your face, except it was covered with cracks. Nothing bloody or gross, not like open wounds or anything. But there were cracks running everywhere. Like when you break a piece of china and you glue all the pieces back together. That's what it was like."

She stopped and looked at me. I said, "Go on."

"But you didn't seem to be in pain. In fact, you were laughing. Just like your old self, chattering and laughing. And then I heard a voice in my dream, and it said, *This is as good as it gets.*"

Her eyebrows knit together. "I wasn't sure if I should tell you . . ."

But I was smiling. "You said I was laughing?"

"Sure. Laughing. But I don't want the dream to scare you or anything, so that's why I—"

I was grinning now. "I was actually laughing."

"Yes. Laughing. But—"

"Mama, that dream doesn't scare me at all. In fact, it encourages me. Know why? Because I'd been broken, but I was still laughing. I'm not afraid of scars. Pain sort of terrifies me, but scars? I can handle those. And I was laughing? Wow. I can definitely handle that."

Cracked but laughing. Imperfect but hopeful. Flawed but happy. Broken but optimistic. Wounded but healing. Scarred but still capable of embracing joy.

There's a certain magic in the way God takes ordinary, imperfect things and uses them in an extraordinary fashion. After all, this is the God who transformed mud into man, water into wine, and barnyard straw into the cradle of a King. And when he manages to turn mourning into laughter, hurting into healing, and wounds into wisdom, well . . . there's magic there, too. And it's a kind of magic I wouldn't know if I'd never gotten broken in the first place.

Scarred . . . but laughing.

Maybe my mom was right. Maybe this is as good as it gets.

And know what? Maybe that's alright with me.

Karen Linamen is the author or coauthor of nine books and a frequent speaker at church and community women's events. She lives with her family in Littleton, Colorado.

To obtain information about having Karen speak at an event, contact Michelle Willett at ConnectionPointe Publicity Resources, michelle@michellewillett.com.

To get in touch with Karen (she always loves hearing from readers!), write to her at karen@karenlinamen.com.

If you liked *Sometimes I Wake Up Grumpy*, you'll love more by this best-selling author!

WARNING: Step away from the chocolate! These joy boosters, stress busters, and hope builders are perfect for all women who fear their mocha desires could be slightly dangerous.

Life is required.
Sanity is optional.

Is there *udder chaos* in your life?

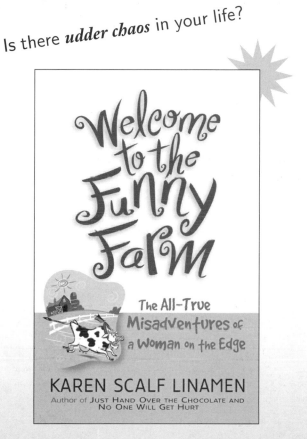

You'll feel better after a trip to the Funny Farm!
With everything from well-woman exams and holiday may-
hem to chocolate binges and a dehydrated gecko, you'll have
an outrageously good time with these insights and practical
advice from the perspective of a woman on the edge.

More advice on marriage and parenthood from Karen Scalf Linamen

True or false: You are what you eat? Find out the answer to this and more common clichés.

You worry about your kids. Let Karen Scalf Linamen show you how to protect them through the power of prayer.

Romance can take a lot of work—and be a lot of fun. With warmth and wit, Karen Scalf Linamen offers a fresh look at enjoying intimacy in your marriage.